BE TRUE TO YOUR FUTURE

Practical Steps to Career Success and Personal Fulfillment

Elwood N. Chapman

CRISP PUBLICATIONS, INC.
Los Altos, California

BE TRUE TO YOUR FUTURE:

Practical Steps to Career Success and Personal Fulfillment

Elwood N. Chapman

CREDITS
Editor: **Michael G. Crisp**
Designer: **Carol Harris**
Typesetting: **Interface Studio**
Cover Design: **Carol Harris**

Copyright © 1988 by Crisp Publications, Inc.
Printed in the United States of America

Crisp books are distributed in Canada by Reid Publishing, Ltd., P.O. Box 7267, Oakville, Ontario, Canada L6J 6L6.

In Australia by Career Builders, P.O. Box 1051 Springwood, Brisbane, Queensland, Australia 4127.

And in New Zealand by Career Builders, P.O. Box 571, Manurewa, New Zealand.

Library of Congress Catalog Card Number 87-73559
Chapman, Elwood N.
Be True To Your Future
ISBN 0-931961-47-5

FROM THE AUTHOR

BE TRUE TO YOUR FUTURE is a life planning book for all ages and most career situations. It contains material from three successful self-study booklets published by Crisp Publications. These are: CAREER DISCOVERY, I GOT THE JOB!, and PLAN B: PROTECTING YOUR CAREER FROM THE WINDS OF CHANGE.

BE TRUE TO YOUR FUTURE can be used in different ways. For example, it is an ideal text for a variety of guidance or adult education courses. It can also be used one-on-one, between a professional counselor and client; and since it is ''self-study'', it can be read by anyone looking for a job, making a career decision, changing careers, or planning for retirement from a primary job. It also will be a major addition to any library, whether on campus, in industry or at home.

The author recommends that the reader become acquainted with all parts of the book and then concentrate on the section that addresses his or her most immediate needs (career search, job search or career change). Sooner or later, after a life goal has been established, all sections of this book will come into play.

Good luck!

Elwood Chapman

E. N. Chapman

ACKNOWLEDGEMENTS

I would like to thank members of the Seal Beach, California, Life Guard staff for reviewing, field testing and contributing ideas to this volume. I also appreciate the contributions of Herff Moore, Bob Maddux and Lee Smith.

I am especially grateful to Mike Crisp for his willingness to accept the idea of three separate books as forerunners to this major effort. The concept of a ''single family'' reference book to help members of all ages be true to their future required support. It was given freely and with enthusiasm.

Thanks also to Carol Harris for her clever, unifying, cover designs.

Elwood N. Chapman

CONTENTS

HITCH YOUR FUTURE

TO A

STAR

> "There is only one success—to be able to spend your life in
> your own way."
>
> *Christopher Morley*

DARE TO DREAM

How can you be true to your future if you don't know what it holds? Good question! Although the future is unpredictable, everyone can have a direct influence on how things turn out. The most successful individuals understand the importance of having a plan which will help them accomplish their dreams. Unfortunately, a majority of individuals seem to exist on a day to day basis. To these people, life consists of "marking time".

Although planning for the future is always tentative, without a plan, there is less chance of a dream coming true. Thus it is important when planning your future to include some high expectations, even though they may appear slightly out of reach. If you do not set your goals high, you may miss out on some great life experiences.

This publication dares you to dream. Then, as a major step to fulfillment, you will be presented with a career discovery strategy that works, a job-hunting system that produces results, and a Plan B that will protect your career from the winds of change. *Be True to Your Future* can benefit a mid-life individual preparing for retirement as much as a student preparing to graduate from college. All you need is a pencil and some time.

Good luck!

START OUT THINKING BIG

One reason people find it so difficult to discover the right career, find the best job, or provide for career growth is because they do not link these efforts to a life goal. Without developing a "larger picture" they drift around like a space ship without a booster rocket.

Trying to discover a suitable career without knowing what you want to do with your life is like taking a trip into a large city without a road map. Hunting for a job without a defined purpose can give a prospective employer the impression you are at loose ends and disorganized. Attempting to achieve successful career growth and protecting it from the winds of change will probably not be realized unless it is part of a larger goal.

Isolating the right life goal for you is not easy or automatic. What is required is concentration and a road map. This book will provide the map if you furnish the concentration.

A good way to begin is to stop looking at college degrees, career possibilities, or job opportunities as ends in themselves. Rather, they should be viewed as vehicles to take you where you really want to go. At first, this may seem overwhelming, but all it really means is that you need to refocus your present thinking. You need to think beyond a degree, a career, or a job. You need to think bigger.

PRACTICAL GOALS ARE BEST

One should avoid coming up with a life goal that is too nebulous to be of use. To be beneficial a goal should be sufficiently clear and strong to establish a set of priorities that provides both direction and enthusiasm.

Please do not get the idea that to be worthwhile your life goal must be highly altruistic or euphoric. Very few individuals will make a significant scientific discover, win a Nobel prize, or be voted most valuable player of a professional sports team. Your realistic life goal may be very practical. It could be:

• raising a happy family in a wholesome environment,

   • buidling your dream home from scratch,

      • improving personal health (longevity) for yourself and your family,

         • having a career that makes other people happy,

            • achieving recognition through creative efforts,

               • creating an estate, or

                  • preparing for a carefree retirement.

LIFE GOALS DIFFER FROM OTHER GOALS

The ideal life goal will provide inspiration over a lifespan. It can be a daily "booster shot" to one's attitude. While a life goal might be gaining recognition from others through a significant achievement; more frequently it is something more personal. Those lucky enough to have a meaningful life goal seem to have more spirit, substance, and direction in their daily lives. And when a crisis occurs, they seem to handle it better than those without a life goal.

It is easy to confuse a life goal with other worthy aspirations. For example, earning a college degree is a significant accomplishment, however it is not normally a life goal. Buying a home is also a worthy objective, but unless there are some special circumstances (like designing and building it yourself) it is not, for most people, a life goal.

You may have thought of a career and life goal as one and the same. This is not always so. In the case of teaching, it might be said that teaching is a career but the life goal (the bigger concept) is a desire to help others learn. A life goal is usually expressed as something more personal and beyond the framework of a career. Often when one chooses a career as a life goal, something is missing. When the career ends, life may not have the meaning the person hoped to enjoy.

CAREER GOALS CAN BECOME LIFE GOALS

For some individuals a career goal can develop into a life goal. When this happens, it is a fortunate occurrence.

George, in his early years, became so involved in becoming a lawyer that he didn't pay any attention to life goals. His passion to become a successful lawyer was all that mattered. Fortunately, some years after he started his practice, George discovered that helping older people was something he really wanted to do. As a result, George changed his practice to specialize in estates and trusts. This allowed him to make a more significant contribution directly helping others. His early career choice eventually led him to his life goal.

Of course, it works both ways. Sometimes a life goal will lead an individual to the best career.

So which should come first?

The premise of this book is that as difficult as it may be to accomplish, the identification of a life goal should come first. This is because such a discovery can motivate an individual to make the best possible career search. People like George (in the situation above who knew early in life what he wanted to be) are in the minority. Most of us need some inspiration to help us complete a career search and job-finding campaign. Having a life goal will motivate us and make our career choice more valid.

BRINGING YOUR LIFE INTO FOCUS

Most people genuinely desire a life goal. They *want* something beyond a career or a job.

Seldom do life goals come easy. Most of us will ultimately succeed achieving a life goal if we stick with it, because life goals are within most of us. They are *there* if we can find a way to bring them to the surface. To help you do this, answer this question:

> WHAT DO YOU REALLY WANT TO ACCOMPLISH THAT WILL GIVE YOU A SENSE OF LASTING FULFILLMENT?

Another approach is to project yourself into the future and imagine you are looking back on your life. Then ask yourself:

> WHAT COULD I HAVE DONE THAT WOULD HAVE GIVEN MY LIFE MORE MEANING?

Because life goals are personal, you may or may not want to share the answers to the above questions with others. Often, however, an open discussion with an appropriate person may help bring your goal or goals into focus.

Although it may be ideal to think about life goals as always being worthy or contributing to humanity, this is not always the case. Some goals, such as accumulating personal wealth, or achieving great power are not altruistic. Yet these can be life goals, because they are highly motivating to some people over an extended period of time.

THE LIFE GOAL CHOICE IS YOURS ALONE

No other person can define a life goal for you or impose one on you. Your goal must come from within. In reality, it is not so much what your stated goal may be as much as the motivation it gives you to make the most of your life. Sadly, even though we only pass through this life once, many of us will never take the time to identify a life goal. Thus most of us drift, or plod. And find less fulfillment.

The following life goal profiles were developed to help you begin a process of isolation and clarification leading to your life goal. It does this by providing examples of how other people came up with life goals and how this discovery helped them select an appropriate career. As you proceed, remember that minds are like parachutes—they don't function until they are open.

LIFE GOAL PROFILES (Continued)

Following are seven examples that illustrate the significant relationship between life goals and career choice. Please ☑ the three with which you most closely identify.

☐ More than anything Jake wants money. Having grown up lacking material goods, Jake sincerely wants financial security and an affluent lifestyle. So strong is his desire, that he intends to remain single until his goal is well on the way to reality. Although some of Jake's friends consider him to be narrowminded and selfish, his goal motivated him to do a comprehensive career search, become a CPA, and accumulate more wealth than any of his old friends. Jake makes no apologies.

☐ Freda has two life goals. One is to travel; the other is to promote international understanding. Freda struggled over a long period of time to reach her goals. As a result, she was almost 40 when she became a travel agent. Thanks to ongoing courses, Freda was bilingual. During her travels, Freda works hard at being a "good will ambassador." Freda tells her friends: "Everything fell into place when I discovered something bigger to devote my life to. I wish I had concentrated on finding a good life goal sooner."

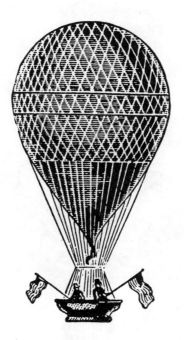

LIFE GOAL PROFILES (Continued)

☐ Jennifer aborted two or three career search efforts and drifted from one job to another for ten years. Nothing came into focus. Then she met a special man and became a born again Christian. This provided her with the insight and motivation to find a career with meaning. Today Jennifer is married to her special man and is a happy, respected professional youth leader in a large midwestern church.

☐ When Mark and Julie ended their marriage, Julie's goal was to be a good parent and provider for their son Jimmy. With help from a college guidance center, she decided to find a career that allowed her to work at home. Computer programming was a perfect solution. Julie was able to find a job that had stability, good income, and allowed her to work at home so she could be with her son. It is a great career with future possibilities, all because Julie put Jimmy first.

☐ Raymond completed two years of college before "stopping out" to do a hitch in the Marine Corps. Following his discharge, he worked in construction as a laborer for three years. He never gave much thought to a career. Then he met Sue. For the first time in his life he wanted a family centered future. By the time they became engaged, Raymond had decided he wanted to complete his college education and become an engineer.

☐ Jose learned from an elementary school teacher that he had artistic talent. Later, even though he was encouraged to continue his education, Jose became a high school drop out. After moving from one unfulfilling job to another, he decided there was more to life. Then he met a Hispanic artist who made a good living through his art. Jose decided he could do as well and made the artist a role model. He returned to school and today Jose is a successful commercial artist and is frequently invited back to his old school as a speaker.

☐ After 25 years as a long-haul truck driver, Jack was forced to quit because of a back injury. For two years he lived off of his disability payments and showed little interest in the future. Then he and his wife were invited to take a trip in an R.V. by friends. The experience was so much fun that Jack and his wife came up with a life goal: to buy an R.V. and build a retirement plan around it! This motivated Jack to accept a job selling R.V.'s. He became so good at it, he now is part owner of a very successful R.V. dealership.

LIFE GOALS CAN CHANGE

Like career choices, or jobs, life goals are not frozen in cement. Although the vignettes in the life goal profiles demonstrated that powerful goals often surface, it does not mean one might not give way to another at a later date. Life goals need to be reviewed, maintained, restored, and sometimes replaced.

Before you engage yourself in other parts of this book, it is important to establish at least a tentative life goal. It need not fully satisfy you at this time, but at least it should assist you to find your best possible current career choice, job, or "Plan B." Should you discover a more significant life goal later, nothing has been lost. In many situations one career has a way of complimenting or leading to another.

On the following page is a diagram. Please complete it. The large star in the middle contains spaces for three life goals. Write in one, two or three.

Once you have recorded your goal or goals you have written the first page of your career script.

GIVE IT YOUR BEST SHOT

TIE CAREER ACTIVITIES TO LIFE GOALS

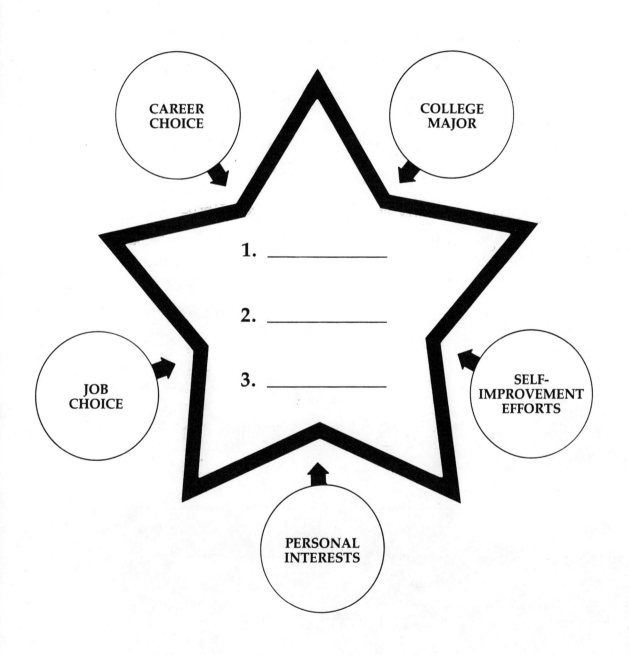

CAREER
CHOICE

COLLEGE
MAJOR

JOB
CHOICE

SELF-
IMPROVEMENT
EFFORTS

PERSONAL
INTERESTS

1. _____

2. _____

3. _____

BOOK ONE

CAREER

DISCOVERY

WRITE YOUR OWN CAREER SCRIPT

Be True to Your Future

''How did I get here? Somebody pushed me. Somebody must have set me off in this direction and clusters of other hands must have touched themselves to the controls at various time, for I would not have picked this way for the world.''

Joseph Heller

PART 1

KNOWING YOURSELF

Be True to Your Future

WHAT ROLES WILL YOU PLAY IN LIFE?

In a very real sense, you write your own script in life. This is because you have considerable freedom to select one career or job over another. You can also become the producer and director of your script. If you wish you can write yourself in as a star; or if you desire a less conspicuous role as a bit player. The choices are many and they are all yours. Exciting!

In the past it was normal for college students to declare a major related to a career; complete a prescribed curriculum of studies; find a job in that field; and often stick with it until retirement. One decision and that was it! Today it is far more common for people to change their majors, do several career searches, (and changes) in a lifetime. Some change careers because they did not make a wise choice initally; others because the one they selected has become obsolete or unsatisfactory; and still others want to match their changing values against a new career possibility.

A career search should not be confused with job-hunting. Finding the right career is an inward search. Finding the right job within a career is a totally different process and will be presented beginning on page 77. A career search requires a demanding exploration which will direct you to selected academic or vocational training or education. In contrast, job-finding is an outward search. One makes an expedition into the world of work to find the best job available within a given career choice. Discovering and qualifying for a career can take years; getting the best job in a chosen area can, with luck, be accomplished in a few weeks. Job-hunting is, in effect, an appendage to a more complicated and extensive previous career search.

WHY A CAREER SEARCH WILL HELP YOU KNOW YOURSELF BETTER

When you look inward and search for a career choice you are also searching for your true identity. You are (perhaps without being aware of it) trying to define who you are, because the more you know about yourself, (traits, characteristics, differences) the better you can project yourself into a suitable career role.

Greg made an attempt at a career search before he dropped out of college and joined the Air Force. He made little progress. After four years, shortly before his discharge, he completed a successful search. The difference? Greg went through considerable introspection and "growing up" in the service. As a result, the second time around he knew himself better and knew what he really wanted. It was much easier for Greg to project himself into a comfortable career.

After her divorce, Macy went through an identity crisis. She became confused about her future and lost her confidence. It took help, but Macy came out of professional counseling knowing herself far better. Earlier, in trying to decide on a career she became frustrated and backed away. This time she followed a logical career search (similar to the one presented in this book) with confidence and found a career that was in harmony with the "real" Macy.

LOOKING AHEAD

Greg and Macy demonstrate that the more you know about yourself the easier and more successful a career search should be. Of course, maturity cannot be forced, but you *can* take time to use certain psychological instruments to help you look closely at who you are and what you want to be. A professional guidance counselor (in your local community college for example), can administer certain testing instruments and help you project ahead to when you are a more ''mature'' person for career purposes. This is what they are trained to do.

As you engage in a search process (either with or without a professional counselor) keep in mind that nothing will work well unless you are honest with yourself. Only you know your values and only you know what will make you happy. It is also essential for you to acknowledge you are primarily responsible for your career script. It would be depressing to wind up at age sixty and realize you spent your working life producing the wrong movie. Do not let others assume the responsibility that belongs to you. Choosing a career is your decision and your opportunity. Only you can be true to your future.

> ''If one advances confidently in the direction of his dreams, and endeavors to live the life which he has imagined, he will meet with success unexpected in common hours.''
>
> *Henry David Thoreau*

WHAT VALUES WILL YOU FEATURE?

A value is a personal standard that you feel to be extremely important. For example, a career that allows you freedom on a daily basis may be more important to you than achieving status from peers. Thus you should consider a career that is less confining over one that provides high recognition but close supervision. Perhaps helping others (showing compassion for those less fortunate) is more important for you than money. If so you probably would prefer a career that provides opportunities to counsel and help others even though the pay may be modest.

Think of values as precious jewels that can adorn and enhance your life. Your values make you unique. When you are true to them, you are in harmony with yourself. Values should be worn quietly and with style.

Values need to be given high priority because when they are compatible with a career choice, you are getting a signal that you will be happy and successful in that particular career. This means that (as far as possible) you should recognize your primary values before undertaking a career search. Easy to say but sometimes difficult to accomplish.

Doing the exercise on the following page will help you clarify your values. The idea is to get you to identify your *three most basic values*. These will be important to take with you during your career search.

GET IN TOUCH WITH YOUR VALUES

This exercise is designed to help you identify your primary values. Please place a ☑ in the appropriate square. Once you have finished, circle three from the ''very important'' column that you intend to keep in mind during your search.

Values	Very Important	Somewhat Important	Not Important
Being free.	☐	☑	☐
Helping others.	☐	☑	☐
Making money.	☑	☐	☐
Working outdoors.	☐	☑	☐
Having a steady job.	☑	☐	☐
Having people respect me.	☑	☐	☐
Having my kind of lifestyle.	☑	☐	☐
Opportunity to learn.	☑	☐	☐
Working regular hours.	☑	☐	☐
Achieving my creative potential.	☐	☑	☐
Experiencing career fulfillment.	☑	☐	☐
Working with people I like.	☑	☐	☐
Doing technical work.	☐	☑	☐
Exhibiting leadership.	☐	☑	☐
Putting my personal life ahead of my job.	☐	☑	☐
Living where I want to live.	☐	☑	☐

My three ''most important'' values are:

1. _M_____
2. _H_____ en_____
3. _E_____ee_____ f_____

> **If you do not remain true to those values you checked ''very important'' you may make the wrong career choice.**

| CASE #1 | Most individuals eventually discover there are tradeoffs between career and lifestyle. Few find careers which blend perfectly. Most must learn to balance both worlds—this usually means compromising. |

A PROBLEM FOR JOYCE

Joyce is an outstanding organizer. For example, in high school, she organized a campaign that won her the position of student body president. She loves to manage and motivate people. Leading others is a thrill. Joyce has decided to become a Business Administration major and try her luck as a manager.

There is only one problem with her major. Joyce also loves animals. So much, in fact, that she has seriously considered becoming a veterinarian. In addition, she feels more comfortable in a rural setting. She seems happier when she is on her parent's farm with the horses, dogs and other animals.

The conflict is obvious. Joyce has always pictured herself living in a country setting surrounded by animals. A job as an executive would probably mean living in a big city and likely moving from time to time. She has heard over and over that to become an executive she must be willing to change organizations when required, work long hours and put her work over her personal lifestyle.

Joyce is a college sophomore so there is plenty of time for her to switch majors.

What would you suggest for Joyce? Should she continue to seek a career in business or should she explore becoming a veterinarian? Can she have a successful career as an executive and still have the lifestyle she wants? Write your opinion in the spaces below and compare with that of the author on page 211.

Open her own store of Animals

_____

_____

_____

YOUR INTERESTS NEED TO BE CONSIDERED

An interest is a curiosity you possess about certain aspects of your environment. Although you may have various degrees of interest in many things, there are probably a few areas where your interest is more intense and lasting. These high level interests will influence your career choice. A keen interest in people has led many to a successful career as a teacher or counselor; a deep interest in the wilderness has produced some professional foresters; an early and consistent interest in reading and books has developed some outstanding librarians.

The special interests you can identify should be given consideration (along with your values) when making a career choice. There are some excellent Interest Inventories (such as the Strong-Campbell or Kuder DD) that will help you pinpoint and rank your interests. These inventories are based on years of research and have proven to help a person select a career where he or she is happy. You are encouraged to take an interest inventory. These are available at almost all college guidance centers for a very modest price. You should then have it interpreted for you by a guidance professional at the location where you are tested. What you learn could be extremely rewarding.

For the purposes of this investigation, please list what you believe to be your top three primary and permanent interests. Do this now.

1. Work w/ hands & machines

2. work w/ people

3.

P.S. It will be interesting for you to compare what you listed above with the results of an interest inventory (if you take one). You might be surprised.

GIVE APTITUDES YOU POSSESS TOP BILLING!

Aptitude implies a natural inclination for a particular kind of work. Translated, this means an ability to quickly master a particular skill.

> As a child, Gus had fun "tinkering" with his toys. He helped his dad do automobile repairs before he had his drivers license. Later Gus found math to be his favorite course. When he did a career search Gus looked for opportunities to capitalize on his special aptitude. No one was surprised when he became a mechanical engineer.

> Gretchen learned to operate a personal computer far ahead of her classmates. She not only took to the keyboard and word processor quickly, Gretchen also enjoyed words, sentence construction, and became excellent at spelling. When it came time to select a career, she was quickly drawn to the office occupation area.

Various aptitude tests are available in most career centers. The mechanical and clerical instruments are the most popular. Should you score high in an aptitude test, it suggests you will have a high probability of success in those careers where that aptitude is important.

If you feel you have a high clerical, mechanical or other aptitude place a ☑ in the appropriate square, then arrange to take a test to confirm your feelings.

       ☐ Mechanical aptitude

       ☐ Clerical aptitude

       ☐ Others: _____

              _____

              _____

SPOTLIGHT YOUR SPECIAL TALENTS

Talents are often confused with aptitudes. We define a talent as a superior, often natural, ability. Talents cover a wide variety of fields. Talent is easy to identify in areas such as the arts or athletics. When people refer to the talent of another, they often use the word "gift". Examples of special talents include outstanding singing or speaking voice, an ability to act, sculpt, play a musical instrument, draw, paint, write, run, throw, kick, jump, hit a ball, swim, etc.

When Marise first started to ice skate she sensed she had more talent than her friends. Recognizing this early, Marise was motivated to devote hours to practice her skills. Through the support of teachers and family members, she became a professional skater and skating instructor.

Geraldine had been in the church choir for only two practice sessions when the leader complimented her on her clear, unusual voice. Ten years (and many voice lessons later) Geraldine became a popular "rock" singer.

Some people tie a lifelong career to a single talent. A few succeed, but many fail and eventually suffer burnout or disappointment. To guard against this, these individuals might consider different ways to use their special talent in *several* career possibilities.

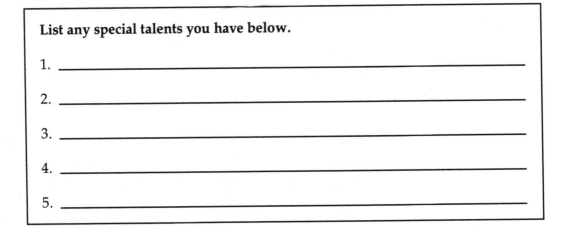

List any special talents you have below.

1. _____

2. _____

3. _____

4. _____

5. _____

YOU CAN'T WRITE A SUCCESSFUL CAREER SCRIPT WITHOUT KNOWING YOUR VALUES, INTERESTS, APTITUDES, TALENTS AND ABILITIES.

BE ALL THAT YOU CAN BE!

In choosing a career, both physical and mental ability should be considered. Top high school and college athletes (in concert with their coaches) need to assess their physical abilities as a prelude to a possible career in professional sports. Other students (through grades and competitive tests) receive signals on how they rank in mental ability compared to others.

The expression "you can be anything you want to be" is not true. For example, only a tiny fraction of athletes are good enough to become a professional basketball player. Not everyone can pass a bar exam regardless of how much formal education they receive, or how many times they take the examination. It is important to be realistic about our ability to succeed in certain careers.

On the other hand, some people do not live up to their potential. We refer to these individuals as underachievers.

> Casey neglected to complete work he was easily capable of doing while in high school. As a result he spent ten years in a menial job. Casey has since returned to school (evening program) and is now a successful small business owner.

Some of us try to reach beyond our capabilities and create unnecessary pressures on ourselves. We refer to these individuals as overachievers.

> Barbara decided in high school to become a research chemist and spent the next eight years trying to qualify without success. Her extreme efforts almost resulted in a nervous breakdown. Thanks to a sensitive counselor, Barbara was channeled into a less demanding career where she uses chemistry and enjoys a high degree of satisfaction.

Everyone needs to find a career that challenges them physically or mentally but, at the same time, falls within their "range".

Name a career beyond your physical or mental ability: _Chemist, football_

Name a career beneath your physical or mental ability: _Mechanic, clerical, sales_

CASE #2	Finding a career is one thing—knowing you can qualify educationally is something else. It is vital you select a career that is within your academic range.

JAKE'S DILEMMA

Jake is totally discouraged because of a conversation he had yesterday with his engineering professor. The instructor called Jake into his office after giving him a failing grade on the midterm examination and said: "Jake, I'm afraid you may be on the wrong educational track. Engineering is a tough discipline and to make it, you must be academically sound in mathematics. If you stay in class, you will need to arrange for tutorial help. My feeling, however, is that you should drop out now, before you have too much invested and move into something less demanding."

Jack is 28 years old and has six years of military training behind him. His years in the Navy convinced him he had excellent mechanical aptitudes. He proved he can repair almost anything. This was what made him elect to choose engineering as a degree choice. Jake's aptitude may be more in engineering application than theory. Some of his friends, for example, have encouraged him to change from electrical engineering to civil engineering.

Yesterday Jake met with his academic counselor who made three suggestions. First, Jake should be honest with himself. In addition to the F in the engineering midterm, Jake is doing poorly in chemistry. Second, Jake should investigate alternative academic courses. Third, if Jake is determined to become an electrical engineer, he should accept tutoring plus an additional year in college for basic remedial work in order to make the transition to a full engineering program.

Will Jake eventually become a degreed engineer? Write your opinion in the spaces below and compare with that of the author on page 211.

to study civil engineer

YOUR WORKING ENVIRONMENT

Your values, interests, aptitudes, talents, and physical/mental abilities are extremely important. The environment under which you must perform also deserves consideration. Would you be happy working 40 hours of shift work each week in a hospital? How about being confined to a science laboratory? Would you be comfortable wearing a uniform each day in a military environment?

Angie became so involved becoming an outstanding computer analyst and advanced programmer that she neglected to think ahead about *where* she could start her career and under what conditions. Upon graduation, the only place where her abilities could be challenged was a computer center in an urban area. Result? A one hour commute, crowded office and a pace she did not anticipate. After two years, Angie accepted a less challenging job to get the kind of slower paced work environment she wanted.

In choosing a career, it is important to consider the following factors:

(1) The physical environment (i.e. type of office, location, parking, and the amount of freedom provided).

(2) People associations. Must you work as a team? Will you be with people you enjoy? Would you prefer to work alone?

(3) What about hours of employment? Will the environment be detrimental to your lifestyle and life goals?

Please list your ideal working environment preferences below:

_____

_____

Please list any working environments you would refuse to accept:

_____ ____ Extensive traveling, Stress situations, pressure _____

_____

THE HAPPINESS FACTOR

Many people believe that if an individual can find a career (or careers) that makes him or her happy, everything else will take care of itself. The rationale goes like this: If you are happy you will automatically do a better job and this will eventually give you the recognition, money, power, personal satisfaction, and anything else you might want. In short, just find a career that will make you happy and you have it made.

The statement, like so many generalizations, does contain at least a kernel of truth. If you find a career that will make you happy, your chances of success are much improved. But happiness is a relative thing. Your career choices should be involving, in harmony with your personal values, and contribute to a purposeful and happy life. They will probably not lead you into a state of euphoria. In short, you may have to be satisfied with something less than pure happiness. An individual who achieves 80 percent job satisfaction is doing exceptionally well.

Generally speaking, finding a career that will make you happy is a matter of matching and balancing your values, abilities, interests, aptitudes, talents and feelings about your work environment with a particular career. The matter of compensation also deserves consideration. Many people might be happiest in careers such as free-lance writing, doing research in tropical flowers, hot air ballooning, or other exotic choices, but these careers might not produce enough income. Sometimes, in order to be true to your long-term future, compromises must be made during the early years of work. This is why it is essential to balance the various factors (values, interests, etc.) discussed in the previous pages.

Congratulations, you have completed Part I. We hope that you now know yourself somewhat better than when you started this section.

In Part II, you will learn how to conduct an effective career discovery search.

PART 2

CONDUCTING YOUR SEARCH

CAREER GUIDANCE SPECIALISTS FEEL STRONGLY THAT A CAREER SEARCH IS THE BEST INVESTMENT IN TIME A PERSON CAN MAKE. WHEN YOU THINK ABOUT IT—THEY ARE PROBABLY RIGHT!

CASE #3	This case will help you understand some of the diverse elements involved in a successful career search.

WILL JOE FIND THE RIGHT CAREER?

After six weeks at a major university, Joe, a freshman, feels lost and frustrated. Despite working hard, Joe is not sure he is on the right educational track. What if he is taking courses that will lead him to the wrong career?

Although pressed for time, yesterday Joe stopped by the campus career center. He was pleased to find a counselor sincerely interested in helping him. After spending forty minutes talking with the counselor, Joe decided he would do the following before the end of the term.

1. Spend time in the career center looking through materials to see if he could find several realistic career possibilities.

2. Take an interest inventory and have the counselor interpret it for him.

3. Solicit opinions about possible careers from close friends and relatives.

4. Be *totally* honest about what he wants and what he is willing to do to achieve success.

5. Return to the counselor before making any major changes.

If Joe does everything listed, what chance do you feel he has of finding the right career? Place a check in the appropriate square.

EXCELLENT ☒   GOOD ☐   POOR ☐

Please turn to page 211 to compare your answer with that of the author.

LONG VS SHORT CAREER SEARCH

When it comes to finding the best career, three options are available. First, you can simply rely on your intuition and search accordingly. Second, you can do a brief, organized search on your own using this publication as a guide. Finally, you can conduct an extended, in-depth search (often in a class setting) under the guidance of an expert.

If you elect to follow your intuition (option 1) the probability of finding the "best" career is low. You might luck out, but most experts recommend against it. Spending a lifetime in the wrong career is a severe price to pay.

SHORT SEARCH

The advantage of a dedicated short search (as prescribed in this book) is that it can produce an immediate career direction using a tested procedure. True, it may not be as foolproof as a long search, but it is far better than simply relying on your own methods. A "short search" should not be considered a "quick fix." Reading this section may take only about one hour, but the concept has been tested and the results have a reasonable level of reliability. The process is logical, and the step-by-step system has value. Best of all, you can take the results from this section to career guidance specialists for additional support. We recommend this for serious career searches. This book is an important first step toward an in-depth search. So, no matter how you look at it, you have everything to gain and nothing to lose from completing the system. Chances are good that you will find quality career choice options that relate to your life goal. Many readers will feel so good about it that they will begin being true to their future. We hope you find yourself in this group.

A SHORT SEARCH IS A GOOD START

LONG SEARCH

For those with time and dedication, an in-depth search is highly recommended. Finding the best career *is* a complex undertaking but something that can affect how happy your life will be. It should be worth whatever time is required to make the best possible career choice.

Where can you start your serious search? Almost all colleges have a 1 or 2 unit career exploration program under the direction of a career professional. These courses can last a full term (normally one or two hours per week). Most will involve taking a series of testing instruments (interest inventories, aptitude tests, personality profiles, etc.). A big advantage in enrolling in such a program is that you receive the psychological support of a guidance expert and can interact with others who are also looking for a career. Those who complete a program not only can end up with one or more exciting career choices, but also benefit from the search itself. Along the way, a person should get to know himself or herself much better.

A long search can also be accomplished on an individual basis under the guidance of a professional. This is often accomplished through the use of a short program which is supplemented with results from various testing instruments, individual counseling, and access to a career center. A career center can provide a wide variety of aids, including some recent sophisticated computerized programs.

Despite all of the help available, it is estimated that only 3% of college students take advantage of career programs. Why this figure is so low is a mystery.

A LONG
SEARCH
IS WORTH
THE
INVESTMENT

BENEFITS FROM COMPLETING A CAREER SEARCH

Place a check in those squares where the statement has high credibility for you.

FINDING YOUR BEST CAREER CHOICE CAN:

☐ Help you achieve a "life goal".

☐ Reduce the frustration that accompanies not knowing what to do with your life.

☐ Help you make the best use of your talents, aptitudes, and abilities.

☐ Motivate you to take advantage of available learning opportunities.

☐ Ultimately increase your income.

☐ Help you better understand "who you are".

☐ Enhance your lifestyle.

☐ Cause you to have more confidence and feel better about yourself.

Are you teaming up with another person in making your search? Testing indicates that the team approach sometimes works well providing that (1) both individuals realize that they are special individuals and therefore have different career needs; (2) they do much of their research independently even though they may be together much of the time; and (3) they are both self-motivated so that if one becomes discouraged and stops, the other one does not automatically follow.

GETTING ON THE RIGHT TRACK

A railroad system has tracks leading in many directions. Each track leads to different stations. Obviously, if you don't get on the right track to start with, you cannot get to the right station without being re-routed.

The same is true in a career search. The most important thing you can do is to get on the right track as soon as possible so that you will wind up at the career station you want. This is especially true when selecting a college major. If you don't choose a major that will lead you to the right careers, (a few years later), you have taken the wrong train.

So what is the answer?

One answer is to identify a few specific career possibilities early and then try to fit them into certain career areas. If enough choices "fit", then you are in a position to select the right track to get there. THIS IS THE SYSTEM USED IN THIS PUBLICATION.

On the following page you are encouraged to list twenty (20) career possibilities for yourself. This may sound like a lot, but it takes that many to make the system work. Do not worry. You will be given all the help required to make your selections. As you do this, keep these two advantages in mind: (1) By stretching your list to twenty possibilities you may discover a career or career area you have neglected in your past thinking. (2) A base of twenty possibilities (you are encouraged to list more) makes the system logical and operative.

This all means that you should be able to find more than one station (specific career) on any track (general career area) you choose to follow. This will give you some significant signals you would not otherwise receive—signals that can reassure you that your search is going in the right direction.

PLEASE TRUST THE SYSTEM AND FOLLOW THE RULES ON THE NEXT PAGE.

TWENTY SPECIFIC CAREER POSSIBILITIES

You have been evaluating career possibilities since you were a child. Some of those which appealed at one time may be more reliable than you think. Reach into your memory and list career possibilities which have potential for you. When you have done this, turn the page and you will receive assistance on how to expand the list to a minimum of twenty.

Career Possibilities	Code Number

1. _Interpreter_ 4,5,1
2. _Commissioner_ 13
3. _Store Manager_ 3
4. _Carpenter_ 7
5. _Auto Body Technician_ 7
6. _Auto Body Repairman_ 7
7. _Electronic Technician_ 7
8. _____ 3
9. _____ 7
10. _____
11. _____ 3
12. _____
13. _____
14. _____ 3
15. _____ 3
16. _____ 5
17. _____
18. _____
19. _____ 2
20. _____ 2

When you have twenty specific career possibilities listed above, please turn to page 45.

To help you find additional career possibilities, more than 200 popular career titles have been listed on the following three pages.* To make your decisions easier, they have been arbitrarily divided into three categories as described below. Please follow directions until you have twenty serious career prospects listed on page 40.

Professional Careers almost always require a college degree. Is your mind geared toward the academic world? Do you enjoy learning? Do you have the self-discipline to complete a university program? Do you have your mind *set* on a four-year degree or beyond? If so, page 42 may contain career ideas that will help you complete your prospect list on page 40. Select only those that have high interest. If you do not find enough to complete your prospect list, investigate the categories below.

Technical Careers are also professional in nature but do not always require a college education. Two years of college or completion of a technical college program is often sufficient. Mechanical and building careers are found in this category. If you are technically or mechanically inclined, turn to page 43 and give the careers listed careful consideration. If possible, select enough to build your prospect list to twenty. Also, explore the service category below.

Service Careers often require a college degree, but not always. These careers offer great opportunity for those who like to work with people. Do you have a desire to serve others? Are people-oriented careers attractive to you? This is an excellent category for highly talented and educated people, but if you do not plan to graduate from a four-year college or university and technical careers have no appeal for you, this category may be your best bet. Please turn to page 44 and attempt to select enough careers from those listed to complete your prospect list on page 40.

(NOTE: Many of the careers listed in one of the above categories could be appropriate for another category. It is of no concern, the idea is to find twenty prospects.)

---

*For an expanded list see the Dictionary of Occupational Titles (DOT) at any library or career center. The DOT is published by the Employment & Training Division of the U.S. Department of Labor.

PROFESSIONAL CAREERS (Partial list)

Circle those that have genuine appeal.

Interpreter 4, 5, 1
Electrical Engineer 6
Dental Hygienist 8
Architect 5, 6
Chemical Engineer 6
Industrial Engineer 6
Aerospace Engineer 6
Home Economist 1, 5, 8
Industrial Designer 5, 6
Clergy 5
Zoologist 9
Journalist 5, 14
Dietician 8
Sanitarian 6
Meteorologist 9, 14
Librarian 5
Registered Nurse 8
Entomologist 9
Oceanographer 9, 14
Mathematician 6, 9, 1
Botanist 9
Lawyer 1, 2, 14
Optometrist 8
Statistician 4, 1, 14
FBI Agent 4
Chiropractor 8
Mechanical Engineer 6
Purchasing Agent 1
Physical Therapist 8
Public Administrator 4
Chemist 9
Sociologist 9, 5, 1
Author 5, 14
Machine Designer 6
Nuclear Scientist 9
Anthropologist 9, 5

Pharmacist 8
Business Administrator 1
Marketing Specialist 3
Forester 10
Actuary 1
Economist 9, 11
Military Officer 11
Teacher 5
Small Business Owner 13
Accountant 1
Banker 1
Psychiatrist 8
Landscape Architect 5, 10
Professional Counselor 5
Physician 8
Youth Leader 5
Dentist 8
Computer Analyst 2
Veterinarian 8
Psychologist 5, 8
Social Worker 4
Civil Engineer 6
Astronomer 9, 14
Computer Programmer 2
Geologist 9
Newscaster 5
Editor 5, 14
Advertising Manager 3, 5
Movie Producer 14, 5
Graphic Artist 5
Laser Specialist 9
Sales Manager 3
Communications Engineer 6
Human Resource Director 1
Certified Public Account 1

Other professional careers:

_____   _____

_____   _____

Add any career possibilities you circled above to those on page 40. Include code numbers.

TECHNICAL CAREER
(Partial list)

Circle those that have genuine appeal.

Surveyor 6, 7, 15
Carpenter 7
Draftsperson 7, 5
Airconditioning Technician 7
Painter - Paperhanger 7
Engineering Technician 7
Railroad Career 15
Automobile Body Repairperson 7
Automobile Mechanic 7
Bricklayer - Stonemason 7
Electronic Technician 7
Broadcasting Technician 7
Television, Radio Repairperson 7
Appliance Repairperson 7
Watch Repairperson 7
Machinist 7
Tool and Die Maker 7
Dental Technician 8
Molder - Coremaker 7
Factory Trainee 7
Medical Technician 8
Pilot 15, 14
Computer Technician 7
Laboratory Technician 8, 7

Airplane Mechanic 7
Diesel Mechanic 7
Millwright 7
Maintenance Electrician 7
U.S. Marines 11
U.S. Army 11
U.S. Air Force 11
U.S. Navy 11
Coast Guard 11
Maintenance Mechanic 7
Firefighter 4
Tilesetter 7
Plasterer 7
Plumber 7
Electrician 7
Business Machines Repairperson 7
Lithographer 5, 7
Forestry Aide 10
Cement Mason 7
Builder 13
Computer Repairperson 7
X-Ray Technician 8
Contractor 13
Barge Operator 14

Additional technical careers:

_____   _____

_____   _____

_____   _____

**Turn to page 40 and list those careers you circled above. Include code numbers.
If you added a career to the list, be sure to include it.**

SERVICE CAREERS
(Partial list)

Circle those that have genuine appeal.

Fashion Designer 14, 5
Actor, Actress 14, 5
Truck, Bus Driver 15
Singer, Dancer, Model 5, 14
Mortician 14
Musician 5
Police Officer 4
Artist 5
Florist 5, 13
Travel Agent 13, 15
Professional Athlete 14
Retail Salesperson 3
Interior Designer 5
Decorator 5
Photographer 5, 13
Telephone Operator 1
Bank Teller 1
News Commentator 5, 14
Traffic Manager 7
Medical Lab Assistant 8
Cosmetologist 5
Automobile Salesperson 3
Guard 15
Restaurant Operator 13
Franchise Owner 13
Para-Medic 8
Museum Guide 14

Insurance Salesperson 3
Supermarket Trainee 15
Professional Salesperson 3
Chef, Cook, Baker 12
Restaurant Manager 12, 13
Waiter/Waitress 12
Bartender 12
Hostess 12
Postal Employee 4
Store Manager Trainee 1
Fashion Salesperson 3
Nurses Aide 8
Flight Attendant 14
Dental Assistant 8
Hotel Career 12
Clerk - Typist 2
Secretary 2
Computer Operator 2
Word Processor 2
Office Manager 2
Practical Nurse 8
Bookkeeper 2, 1
Stock Broker 3
Firefighter 4
Real Estate Salesperson 3
Disk Jockey 14
Hairstylist 5

Other service careers:

_____   _____

_____   _____

_____   _____

Return to page 40 and list those careers you circled above. Include code numbers. If you added a career be sure to list it.

CAREER BOXES:
YOUR SEARCH EXPANDS

By listing a minimum of twenty specific career possibilities on page 40 you have created a base from which you can more rationally determine which career track to take. The system works like this.

Specific careers usually come in clusters. For example, there are many kinds of medical doctors or nurses. These are small clusters. But it is possible to place all medical careers (hundreds) into one big cluster. When an individual shows interest in more than one career that falls within a cluster, this intensifies the interest and is a signal that this individual may be on the right career track.

> Nick independently selected four specific careers that wound up in a single cluster. This made Nick feel great because it was, in a sense, a discovery to realize all were related. Without knowing it, he was leaning in the direction of one career track over the others available.

You will find 15 Career Boxes (clusters) on the following pages. The idea is to assign your twenty specific career choices into the appropriate boxes. This will help you discover which directions you are headed in. The system employed is one of self-discovery.

The process is easy. If a career has a code number (from pages 42, 43, and 44) it should be listed in the box with the same number. In some cases, a specific career may have more than one code number. If so, it should be written in all of the boxes indicated.

If you prefer not to use the code numbers, or you list careers not found on pages 42, 43, or 44, thumb through the career boxes and assign the career to the box you feel is most appropriate. If you do not find a suitable box for a specific career, place it in Box 15 found on page 60.

When each career has been written into the most appropriate box, please turn to page 62.

Career Box #1

GENERAL BUSINESS

(Management, production, warehousing, transportation. Does not include office occupations, sales and marketing, or owning your own business.)

THINK MANAGERIAL AND THE SUPERVISION OF OTHERS. This is the largest of all occupational areas. The work environment is highly competitive. Chances are good you would work for a large organization. Most Business majors fall into this category.

Specific ⟶ 1. _interpreter_
Careers 2. _bank teller_
    3.
    4.
    5.
    6.
    7.
    8.
    9.
    10.

WILL THIS OCCUPATIONAL AREA;

	Yes	No
Measurably help you reach your life goals?	☐	☒
Be compatible with your values?	☐	☐
Capitalize on your special interests?	☐	☐
Challenge your mental abilities?	☐	☐
Take advantage of any aptitudes you were able to identify?	☐	☐
Make use of any special talents you may possess?	☐	☐
Provide the working environment you want?	☐	☐

Career Box #2

OFFICE OCCUPATIONS
(Accounting, secretarial, word processing, office managers, etc.)

THINK OFFICE AUTOMATION. Most employees in this area have basic computer competence and above average English and computational skills. Most jobs are performed within office environments in large cities. Commuting is normal.

Specific ⟶ 1. computer operator
Careers
       2. word processor
       3.
       4.
       5.
       6.
       7.
       8.
       9.
      10.

WILL THIS OCCUPATIONAL AREA;

	Yes	No
Measurably help you reach your life goals?	☐	☑
Be compatible with your values?	☑	☐
Capitalize on your special interests?	☐	☐
Challenge your mental abilities?	☐	☐
Take advantage of any aptitudes you were able to identify?	☐	☐
Make use of any special talents you may possess?	☐	☐
Provide the working environment you want?	☐	☐

Career Box #3

SALES/MARKETING OCCUPATIONS

(Marketing specialists, sales representative for manufacturers, stock brokers and Real Estate professionals, retail sales people etc.)

THINK INTERACTING WITH OTHERS. Individuals in this area are normally out-going and enjoy people. They are also competitive and like daily challenges. They value freedom of movement and don't mind taking risks. Most enjoy the fast lane and are open to job changes.

Specific ⟶ 1.
Careers

2.

3.

4.

5.

6.

7.

8.

9.

10.

WILL THIS OCCUPATIONAL AREA;

	Yes	No
Measurably help you reach your life goals?	☐	☐
Be compatible with your values?	☑	☐
Capitalize on your special interests?	☑	☐
Challenge your mental abilities?	☐	☐
Take advantage of any aptitudes you were able to identify?	☐	☐
Make use of any special talents you may possess?	☐	☑
Provide the working environment you want?	☑	☐

Career Box #4

GOVERNMENT AND SOCIAL SERVICE

(Police force, firefighter, postal employees, welfare counselor, probation officer, unemployment counselor, border patrol, etc.)

THINK CITY, COUNTY, STATE, AND FEDERAL AGENCY. This is an extremely large, diverse, and bureaucratic employment area. Although working environments are highly structured, opportunities are many. Job security and early retirement possibilities exist.

Specific ⟶ 1. _firefighter_
Careers

2. _police officer_

3.

4.

5.

6.

7.

8.

9.

10.

WILL THIS OCCUPATIONAL AREA;

	Yes	No
Measurably help you reach your life goals?	☑	☐
Be compatible with your values?	☑	☐
Capitalize on your special interests?	☑	☐
Challenge your mental abilities?	☑	☐
Take advantage of any aptitudes you were able to identify?	☐	☐
Make use of any special talents you may possess?	☐	☐
Provide the working environment you want?	☑	☐

50

Career Box #5

CREATIVE, EDUCATIONAL, RELIGIOUS
(Educators, teachers, ministers, entertainers, publishers, newscasters, youth leaders, etc.)

THINK VERBAL COMMUNICATIONS. This is generally a high visibility career area where individuals are creative and expressive. Most are leaders and like the feeling of being ''in charge''. Normal working hours are less important than the freedom to be creative.

Specific ──────►1. Interpreter
Careers
2.
3.
4.
5.
6.
7.
8.
9.
10.

WILL THIS OCCUPATIONAL AREA;

	Yes	No
Measurably help you reach your life goals?	☒	☐
Be compatible with your values?	☒	☐
Capitalize on your special interests?	☒	☐
Challenge your mental abilities?	☒	☐
Take advantage of any aptitudes you were able to identify?	☐	☒
Make use of any special talents you may possess?	☐	☒
Provide the working environment you want?	☒	☐

Career Box #6

HIGH TECH/ENGINEERS
(Computer science professionals, scientists, designers, engineers of many kinds, and the technicians that back them up.)

THINK MODERN TECHNOLOGY. This is a difficult occupational area to define but it helps to think of those who design, build, and maintain the complex technology around us. Often the job is in a laboratory environment. High level skills are normally required. Advanced academic degrees are common.

Specific ——→ 1.
Careers

    2.

    3.

    4.

    5.

    6.

    7.

    8.

    9.

    10.

WILL THIS OCCUPATIONAL AREA;

	Yes	No
Measurably help you reach your life goals?	☐	☐
Be compatible with your values?	☐	☐
Capitalize on your special interests?	☐	☐
Challenge your mental abilities?	☐	☐
Take advantage of any aptitudes you were able to identify?	☐	☐
Make use of any special talents you may possess?	☐	☐
Provide the working environment you want?	☐	☐

Career Box #7

TRADES/CRAFTS

(Benchwork occupations, building trades, heavy-equipment operators, contractors, printing and textile occupations, etc.)

THINK BLUEPRINTS AND WORKING WITH YOUR HANDS. Most who select this area have a high mechanical aptitude. They like to see what they build. Many enjoy outdoor work. A sizable percentage work for themselves.

Specific ──────➤ 1. *Carpenter*
Careers

2. *Aviation Tech.*

3. *Auto body repair*

4. *Broadcasting tech*

5. *Computer tech*

6.

7.

8.

9.

10.

WILL THIS OCCUPATIONAL AREA;

	Yes	No
Measurably help you reach your life goals?	☐	☐
Be compatible with your values?	☑	☐
Capitalize on your special interests?	☑	☐
Challenge your mental abilities?	☑	☐
Take advantage of any aptitudes you were able to identify?	☑	☐
Make use of any special talents you may possess?	☐	☑
Provide the working environment you want?	☐	☑

Career Box #8

HEALTH SERVICES
(Doctors, dentists, veterinarians, nurses, paramedics, medical lab assistants, etc.)

THINK WHITE UNIFORMS/HOSPITALS/DENTAL OFFICES/CLINICS.
The work environment of health services is easy to define. Most have a compassion for others and are willing to work odd-hours. Careers include everything from the physician with years of specialized training to a medical clerk just out of high school.

Specific ——→ 1. Med. Tech
Careers

2. Med. Lab. Assistant

3.

4.

5.

6.

7.

8.

9.

10.

WILL THIS OCCUPATIONAL AREA;

	Yes	No
Measurably help you reach your life goals?	☐	☒
Be compatible with your values?	☐	☒
Capitalize on your special interests?	☐	☒
Challenge your mental abilities?	☒	☐
Take advantage of any aptitudes you were able to identify?	☐	☒
Make use of any special talents you may possess?	☐	☒
Provide the working environment you want?	☒	☐

Career Box #9

EARTH, PHYSICAL & BEHAVIORAL SCIENCES

(Biologist, zoologist, chemist, geologist, and other physical scientists; anthropologist, sociologist, political scientists and others attempting to learn more about our history and culture.)

THINK SPECIALIZATION. Here we have a wide variety of professions that often attract those who enjoy research and, at the same time, seek recognition. Many who are interested in this area eventually become teachers.

Specific——→1.
Careers

2.

3.

4.

5.

6.

7.

8.

9.

10.

WILL THIS OCCUPATIONAL AREA;

	Yes	No
Measurably help you reach your life goals?	☐	☐
Be compatible with your values?	☐	☐
Capitalize on your special interests?	☐	☐
Challenge your mental abilities?	☐	☐
Take advantage of any aptitudes you were able to identify?	☐	☐
Make use of any special talents you may possess?	☐	☐
Provide the working environment you want?	☐	☐

Career Box #10

FARMING, FORESTRY, FISHING
(Includes all forms of land cultivation, animal production, mining, and food storage and transportation.)

THINK OUTDOORS. Most people in these careers prefer to be away from crowds. They enjoy being close to nature, are not afraid of hard work, prefer not to be restricted to regular hours, and might opt for a pickup truck rather than an automobile for family use.

Specific ——→ 1.
Careers
        2.

        3.

        4.

        5.

        6.

        7.

        8.

        9.

        10.

WILL THIS OCCUPATIONAL AREA;

	Yes	No
Measurably help you reach your life goals?	☐	☐
Be compatible with your values?	☐	☐
Capitalize on your special interests?	☐	☐
Challenge your mental abilities?	☐	☐
Take advantage of any aptitudes you were able to identify?	☐	☐
Make use of any special talents you may possess?	☐	☐
Provide the working environment you want?	☐	☐

Career Box #11

MILITARY
(All careers found in the Army, Navy, Air Force, Marines, and Coast Guard.)

THINK PATRIOTISM AND DISCIPLINE. Many occupations exist in the field (support services range from office occupations to high technology), it is normally the most structured of environments. Many enjoy the status of a uniform.

Specific ⟶ 1.
Careers
2.

3.

4.

5.

6.

7.

8.

9.

10.

WILL THIS OCCUPATIONAL AREA;

	Yes	No
Measurably help you reach your life goals?	☐	☑
Be compatible with your values?	☑	☐
Capitalize on your special interests?	☑	☐
Challenge your mental abilities?	☑	☐
Take advantage of any aptitudes you were able to identify?	☑	☐
Make use of any special talents you may possess?	☐	☑
Provide the working environment you want?	☐	☑

Career Box #12

HOSPITALITY
(Restaurant, hotel, travel occupations, etc.)

THINK SERVICE AND FRIENDLINESS. When you consider all of the eating places, hotels, resorts, amusement parks and recreational areas you soon realize that hospitality (serving others) is big business and getting bigger. Most who work in this area are people-oriented, willing to work odd hours, and like the lively, sometimes glamorous, atmosphere. Many who start out in a hospitality industry wind up in management positions or ownership roles.

Specific ———→ 1. career
Careers 2.
  3.
  4.
  5.
  6.
  7.
  8.
  9.
  10.

WILL THIS OCCUPATIONAL AREA;

	Yes	No
Measurably help you reach your life goals?	☑	☐
Be compatible with your values?	☐	☐
Capitalize on your special interests?	☐	☐
Challenge your mental abilities?	☑	☐
Take advantage of any aptitudes you were able to identify?	☐	☐
Make use of any special talents you may possess?	☐	☐
Provide the working environment you want?	☑	☐

58

Career Box #13

ENTREPRENEURSHIP

(Owning your own manufacturing, wholesale, or retail business; becoming a franchisee. Operating a special service out of your home.)

THINK FREEDOM: Not everyone is geared to work for another individual or firm. To satisfy their values, some need to operate alone, even though they work harder and more hours than if they were on a payroll. Almost all of the career boxes listed (15) provide learning experiences that can lead to entrepreneurship.

Specific ———→1.
Careers

2.

3.

4.

5.

6.

7.

8.

9.

10.

WILL THIS OCCUPATIONAL AREA;

	Yes	No
Measurably help you reach your life goals?	☐	☒
Be compatible with your values?	☐	☒
Capitalize on your special interests?	☐	☐
Challenge your mental abilities?	☐	☐
Take advantage of any aptitudes you were able to identify?	☐	☐
Make use of any special talents you may possess?	☐	☐
Provide the working environment you want?	☐	☐

Career Box #14

UNUSUAL, EXOTIC OCCUPATIONS

(This category includes everything from being a curator in a museum, a singing messenger, to a dance therapist).

THINK DIFFERENT. Nobody can keep up with new careers that spring up daily in our society. Some people create their own jobs by doing something others have not thought of doing such as selling "pet rocks". If the career or job you have in mind does not fit into any of the other categories—and it has an unusual twist to it—consider this career box.

Specific ——→1.
Careers
  2.

  3.

  4.

  5.

  6.

  7.

  8.

  9.

  10.

WILL THIS OCCUPATIONAL AREA;

	Yes	No
Measurably help you reach your life goals?	☐	☐
Be compatible with your values?	☐	☐
Capitalize on your special interests?	☐	☐
Challenge your mental abilities?	☐	☐
Take advantage of any aptitudes you were able to identify?	☐	☐
Make use of any special talents you may possess?	☐	☐
Provide the working environment you want?	☐	☐

Career Box #15

MISCELLANEOUS

WHEN A CAREER DOESN'T FIT EASILY OR COMFORTABLY INTO THE
FIRST FOURTEEN BOXES, PLACE IT IN THIS ONE. This does not mean
that it is a less exciting or unimportant career, it simply means it did not fit
into one of the contrived career boxes.

Specific ⟶ 1. *supermarket trainee*
Careers

2.

3.

4.

5.

6.

7.

8.

9.

10.

WILL THIS OCCUPATIONAL AREA;

	Yes	No
Measurably help you reach your life goals?	☒	☐
Be compatible with your values?	☒	☐
Capitalize on your special interests?	☒	☐
Challenge your mental abilities?	☒	☐
Take advantage of any aptitudes you were able to identify?	☒	☐
Make use of any special talents you may possess?	☐	☒
Provide the working environment you want?	☒	☐

BE SURE YOU ANSWER THE QUESTIONS BENEATH ANY CAREER BOX IN WHICH YOU ENTER A SPECIFIC CAREER POSSIBILITY. THEY WILL HELP YOU DETERMINE WHETHER THAT CAREER CLUSTER IS COMPATIBLE WITH YOUR GOALS, VALUES, INTERESTS, ABILITIES, APTITUDES, TALENTS AND VIEWS ABOUT A WORKING ENVIRONMENT.

SELECTING THE RIGHT CAREER BOX

You may have already decided on the career box that you think is best. The system (assigning specific careers to one of fifteen boxes) often explains itself and further explanation seems redundant. There are, however, a few cautions one might be wise to honor.

ANY CAREER BOX WITH A SPECIFIC CAREER LISTED IS DESERVING OF CONSIDERATION. Sometimes an individual is locked into one or two specific careers and either one or both are the only ones of interest within their best career area.

> Rachel only listed two careers (Registered and Psychiatric Nurse) in the Health Services career box but listed six in the Office Occupations box. Even so, her interest, values and life goals were stronger in Health Services. As a result, she made the right decision when she attended nursing school.

THE CAREER BOX THAT ATTRACTED MOST OF YOUR SPECIFIC CAREER CHOICES SHOULD BE CHALLENGED. Just because one box may have the largest number of specific careers listed does not automatically make it the best choice.

> To his surprise, Josh wound up with seven specific careers in the High Tech/Engineering box. Because of this he was tempted to make a selection out of the seven. However, in discussing his results with a guidance counselor, Josh recognized that his interest in becoming a biologist (Science box) was greater than he thought. The choice was also a better fit as far as his work environment preferences and other factors. His second and third choice, however, came from the High Tech/Engineering box.

SELECTING THE RIGHT CAREER BOX
(Continued)

IT IS A GOOD IDEA TO REVIEW AND COMPARE "YES" AND "NO" ANSWERS IN ALL BOXES WHERE A CAREER WAS LISTED. It is possible that you may wish to do additional research in one career area (box) and want to rethink the potential it may have.

> Brad took time to answer all of the questions at the bottom of each box and discovered that he got more yes answers from the box 13 (Entrepreneurial) than others. This caused him to go back and spend more time on his list of twenty specific careers, making a few revisions. In the end, Brad settled for the Entrepreneurial box and expanded the specific career possibilities.

When the time comes to select the right career box, it is always a good idea to talk things over with another and do some extra thinking.

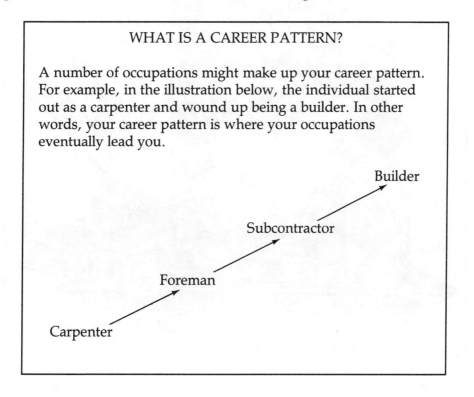

WHAT IS A CAREER PATTERN?

A number of occupations might make up your career pattern. For example, in the illustration below, the individual started out as a carpenter and wound up being a builder. In other words, your career pattern is where your occupations eventually lead you.

Builder

Subcontractor

Foreman

Carpenter

PART 3

SELECTING A SPECIFIC CAREER

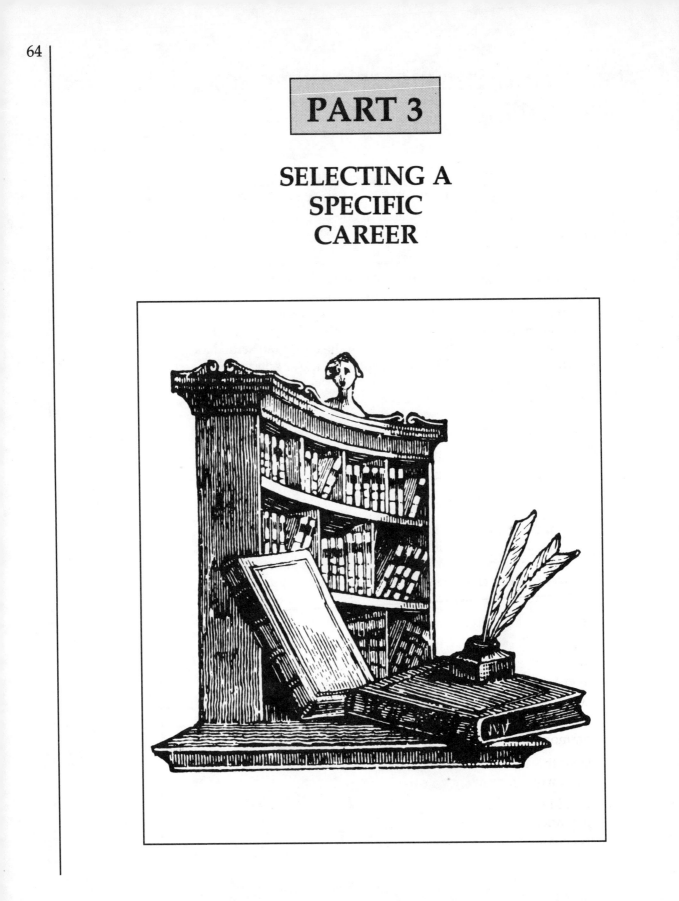

ASKING YOURSELF QUESTIONS

Once you narrow down possible career choices you should learn as much about the career in question as possible. Far too many people commit themselves to a career without doing enough research. If these individuals would spend a few hours in a local library, campus career center, or best of all talking to others who have made a career choice in the same field, they could protect themselves against making a mistake they might regret later. Some career guidance specialists recommend that people do research at the initial point of selection (prospects) and further investigation after narrowing choices to three.

QUESTIONS YOU SHOULD BE ABLE TO ANSWER ABOUT ALL YOUR CAREER PROSPECTS

1. What are the specific training or educational requirements? What kind of training? How much education? Where are the schools located? What will it cost?

2. What other qualifications are needed? Does the career demand a certain trait, skill, or aptitude I do or do not have?

3. What is the nature of the work? Would I like it? Is it the sort of thing I could do over a long period of time?

4. What is the work environment? Is the occupation only in a factory? Office? Outdoors? Indoors? What about the hours?

5. What is the earning potential? Will I be able to make enough money to satisfy myself? Will I reach my salary peak too soon?

6. Where could I find such a job? Only in a big city? Would I like the geographical location?

7. What is the employment outlook? Good? Poor? Will there be openings after I complete my education?

8. Will the career permit me to live the life-style I seek? How much freedom will I have? What are the pressures? Will the job be at least somewhat in harmony with my personal values?

9. Does this career mean I would be forced to work for a big organization? If so, would I be able to cope with it?

10. Would I be successful? Would the career push me to live up to my potential? Or would I be underemployed in a few years?

#ONE RESOURCE BOOK

Locate an *Occupational Outlook Handbook* (OOH) published by the United States Department of Labor. The latest edition should be in any library or career center. It looks like a very large telephone book, and it is the best single source of up-to-date career information. It contains data on most occupations, including nature of work, educational requirements, earnings, conditions of work, and employment outlook. All of this information is vital to the decisions you will make later.

THE PROCESS OF ELIMINATION

The process of elimination is a sound procedure, especially when it comes to choosing a career. When you narrow your choices to a single career box, you have made excellent progress. When you can narrow your choice even further, the results are not only gratifying but probably reliable. Here are three suggestions to assist you in selecting a specific career from the career box you chose.

1. YOU MAY WISH TO DO SOME OUTSIDE RESEARCH TO LEARN MORE ABOUT THE SPECIFIC CAREERS IN YOUR CHOSEN BOX. You could, for example, go to a library or career center and read everything you can find about each career; or you could interview someone already occupying the career; or, if you are on campus, talk with a professor who teaches in the career area chosen.

> Jill had a good feeling about the career box she selected (General Business) but couldn't decide whether she wanted to be a CPA or take a more general course in Business Administration. After doing more reading and talking to her accounting professor she decided on becoming a CPA. Jill's excellent grades in accounting and her side interest in Data Processing helped her make the important decision.

2. ALTHOUGH THE QUESTIONS AT THE BOTTOM OF EACH CAREER BOX CAN BE HELPFUL IN DECIDING WHICH BOX IS BEST, THEY CAN BE OF EVEN MORE HELP IN SELECTING A SPECIFIC CAREER. It is recommended that the reader evaluate each specific career within a box based upon the questions. The one receiving the most yes answers should be given priority consideration.

> Doug was amazed to discover that twelve out of his twenty specific career choices fell into the Creative/Education/Religious box. As he went through the list (asking the seven questions) he discovered that the career of becoming a Journalist rated higher than others. Was he attracted to this career because he was a sports writer in high school? Did it combine all of the creative and educational aspects of other careers? At any rate, Doug decided on the basis of the answers to become a journalism major with a minor in education.

3. WHEN YOU ARE ON THE RIGHT TRACK YOU CAN DELAY SPECIFIC
   CAREER CHOICES UNTIL LATER. It is estimated by experts that 50% of
   those who graduate from college are, by their own admission, in the wrong
   major. This is a signal that they were on the wrong track from the start.

> Because of her high mental ability level, unusual mechanical aptitude,
> and interest in mathematical theory, Angelica knew she had found the
> right career box, but also recognized that it would take more education
> and time before she could make a specific career choice. After discussing
> the matter with her counselor, Angelica decided to spend a full year
> investigating the possibilities. She figured she needed to know exactly
> where she was going before entering graduate school.

DECISION TIME*

If you have conscientiously followed the system presented in the previous pages, you have reached a point where you should be able to make a tentative specific career choice. You may wish further vertification in the future, but for planning purposes you can commit yourself now. In doing this, you are not closing the door on other options. Please write your choice below.

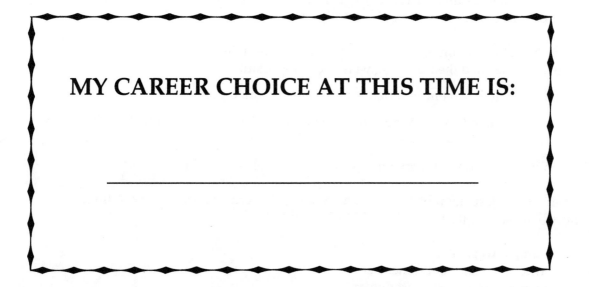

MY CAREER CHOICE AT THIS TIME IS:

_____

---

*If you feel you need additional time to learn more about your leading career possibilities before making a decision, you should delay your decision until such research has been accomplished.

CASE #4

People often experience personal growth and leave unsatisfactory careers behind.

Also dynamic changes in the world of work can make careers obsolete.

That is why you may decide to review the process presented in this program at regular intervals.

MID-LIFE CAREER CHANGE

Richard is happily married with two teen-age children. For the last four years he has felt trapped in his position with a large corporation. There are three primary reasons Richard feels this way. First, the company is not experiencing the growth it experienced in the past. This limits opportunities for promotion. Second, Richard has a negative attitude about his immediate boss; and he knows top management is aware of his feelings. Third, Richard never made a career search and feels his talents have never been fully exploited.

With the help of an understanding wife, Richard has taken a close look at his values. He decided the following were most important.

1. A desire to be an entrepreneur—free from corporate politics.

2. An aspiration to stay in the same geographical area, with the same friends— probably in the same house.

3. A job where he can work with people—especially customers.

After devoting six months to a personal search, Richard has come up with three possibilities. ALL IN THE HOSPITALITY FIELD.

Start a travel agency.
Become a restaurant franchisee.
Manage a motel as a part owner.

How could Richard and his wife verify, ahead of time, they are making the right decision? Write your specific suggestion below.

_____

_____

_____

Compare your opinion with that of the author on page 211.

PART 4

VERIFICATION
OF
CHOICE

SATISFY YOURSELF

It is often difficult to be true to yourself especially when dealing with long term decisions such as your future. So, naturally, the selection of a career that is in harmony with your life goals is a heavy decision. This is why you may wish to take the following suggestions seriously.

Suggestion 1: TALK THINGS OVER WITH OTHERS. All career choices are, in a sense, tentative. You should discuss how you are feeling about possible careers with those close to you so they can either reinforce your feelings or, in some cases, raise questions and concerns.

Suggestion 2: CONDUCT SOME CAREER INTERVIEWS: There is no better way to verify what you have learned or what you anticipate than talking with someone who occupies the career position you are striving to reach. These individuals can usually be found in your own community and all it normally takes to set up an interview is a telephone call.

Suggestion 3: SPEND TIME IN THE APPROPRIATE WORK ENVIRONMENT: In some cases it is possible to get a part-time job or apprenticeship in a career area you wish to investigate. For example, if you were thinking about owning your own restaurant, you might become a waiter/waitress in one similar in size and menu to the one you envision owning. If you were thinking about becoming a nurse, you might work as a volunteer in a hospital or nursing home. Nothing can take the place of actual exposure in advance of a decision.

Suggestion 4: TALK TO A GUIDANCE EXPERT: If you are lucky enough to have a university or community college nearby, go to the guidance or career center and make an appointment to discuss your situation with a counselor. Take the results of your preliminary career search data with you. Ask the person you contact for suggestions on how to verify your choice. Are there any testing instruments that might help? Is there a computer-based program available? What reading is recommended?

As you take advantage of any or all of the above suggestions please keep in mind that when you are true to yourself, your future will often take care of itself.

| CASE #5 | When some people realize how much impact a career choice will have on their lives, they panic and lose confidence in their choice. This is unfortunate because after a good search has been completed—and the individual has a satisfied feeling—that person should usually go with the decision. If necessary, a career change can be made after further personal growth is experienced. |

SECOND THOUGHTS

Mrs. Henderson has conscentiously completed a career discovery program similar to the one in this book. She found it difficult to list enough career possibilities but was able to place three of her choices inside the HEALTH SERVICES box. Her final choice was that of a Psychiatric Nurse.

Now Mrs. Henderson has second thoughts. Looking back over her efforts it all seemed too easy. Did she give sufficient consideration to her values? Did she apply what she learned from the case studies to her own situation? Will she be able to handle the advanced academic training?

Are Mrs. Hendeson's misgivings natural? Is it possible to discover the *right* career so easily and quickly? Should Mrs. Henderson consider her program as only a "starter" and conduct a more in-depth search, using available interest inventories, personality tests, computer data base information, and other materials?

Would taking this program a second time in a few days or a few weeks give Mrs. Henderson more confidence in the system and her decision to become a Psychiatric Nurse?

Please write your answers in the space provided below and compare your answers with those of the author on page 211.

_____

_____

_____

_____

_____

SHOULD YOU CONSIDER A DEEPER SEARCH?

Now that you have completed this short program, should you consider a more extended approach? Should you investigate a regular on-campus career guidance course? The list below is designed to help you make this decision. Please place a check in any square that applies to you.

☐ Taking the short-form program has made me interested in joining a group program (regular class) under the close guidance of a career expert. I feel that the results will be worth the extra investment in time.

☐ I appreciate the career choices from the short-form approach, but the results are not as convincing as I had hoped they might be. I think I need to do a full-fledged search before I will feel secure in my choice.

☐ I really skipped over the short-form program and, as a result, the results may not be as valid as they should be. I need to make a second effort and take it more seriously.

☐ I want more diagnostic assistance. I would like to take a few tests and have them interpreted to help me in my search.

☐ I need to make my search under conditions where I am under less pressure. In a few weeks, the timing will be better.

☐ I need constant support from both a teacher and other students if I am going to make a productive career search.

☐ I have yet to make a firm choice as to my college major and I want a more thorough search to make absolutely certain I am on the right educational track.

☐ The reason I want to become involved in a deeper career search is so I can get to know myself better. Finding the right career is secondary to me.

☐ I need more time to focus on a life goal.

FOLLOW-UP CHECK LIST

Place a mark in the square opposite those action steps you intend to take within the next few weeks.

☐ Discuss the life goal (or goals) I selected on page 13 with a close friend.

☐ Discuss the career choice I made on page 69 with the same friend, another individual, or a family member whose opinion I respect.

☐ Make an appointment with a career counselor to discuss the progress I have made.

☐ If my career selection requires additional formal education, make an appointment with an academic counselor to plan my future educational program.

☐ Discuss my career choice with someone already in the profession or job area.

☐ For validation purposes, wait two weeks and complete this program a second time.

☐ Go on a job-hunting expedition to find an interim position closer to my career choice.

☐ Do some new financial planning (investigating scholarships, borrowing money, working during the summer etc.) to help me reach my new career goal.

TEST YOURSELF

Demonstrate you understand the value of a career search by answering the following true and false questions. Correct answers will be found at the bottom of the page.

True   **False**

_____   _____   1. When tied to life goals, a career search is easier *and* more valid.

_____   _____   2. There is little relationship between a career and personal identity search.

_____   _____   3. Career goals can become life goals.

_____   _____   4. A short career search using a good system will normally produce results equal to a more indepth search.

_____   _____   5. Talents and aptitudes are more similar than interests and abilities.

_____   _____   6. A person considering college needs to do a career search so that she or he can get on the best academic track.

_____   _____   7. Clustering specific career possibilities (chosen in advance) is a good way to verify whether one is heading in the right general direction.

_____   _____   8. Most colleges do not employ professional career specialists.

_____   _____   9. When you tie a career search to a life goal you are being true to your future.

_____   _____   10. By completing this program you have, in effect, started to write your own career script.

ANSWERS: 1. T 2. F 3. T 4. F 5. T 6. T 7. T 8. F 9. T 10. T

B
O
O
K

T
W
O

I GOT THE JOB!

Prospecting Strategies and Interviewing Techniques to Win a Job Your Way

Be Your Own Employment Agency

When you find the *right* job it can support and enhance your lifestyle but it can also provide a kind of happiness not found in your personal life. When this happens, you no longer consider your job activities "work".

It is the purpose of this book to help you *discover* and *win* the best job available within your geographic perimeters. The strategies and techniques presented, however, are designed to help you do it *your* way. That is, you will have full opportunity to put all of your personal creativity into the search and interview process.

Best of all, you can start doing this now. When you turn this page and others you will be able to add to or revise the recommendations as you proceed. Do this! Be your own employment agency! All you need for a great start is a little time and a pencil!

Good luck!

> *"A man's work is his dilemma; his job is his bondage, but it also gives him a fair share of his identity and keeps him from being a bystander in somebody else's world."*
>
> *Melvin Maddocks*

CREATIVE JOB HUNTING

PART 1

ATTITUDE + CONFIDENCE = SUCCESS

WHAT YOU ARE
ABOUT TO LEARN
REGARDING JOB-HUNTING
WILL HELP YOU
BE MORE PROFESSIONAL

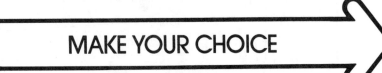

MAKE YOUR CHOICE

MAKE YOUR CHOICE NOW!

CHARACTERISTICS OF SUCCESSFUL JOB SEEKERS	**CHARACTERISTICS OF UNSUCCESSFUL JOB SEEKERS**

Those who remain positive about the challenge.	Those who discourage easily and start looking for excuses.
Applicants who stay with a system that utilizes recognized job-finding techniques.	Job-seekers who do not bother to research firms ahead of interviews.
Those who plan their work and work their plan.	Those who decide making professional use of the telephone is too much trouble.
Those who use "networking" as their primary prospecting strategy.	Applicants who refuse to devote at least 50% of their job-hunting time to prospecting.
Those who study and understand the dynamics of the modern job market.	Those who underestimate the personal contribution to productivity they can make.
	Those who downgrade the importance of keeping a positive attitude.

Add your own ideas here:

_____

_____

_____

Add your own ideas here:

_____

_____

_____

A good job finding process does not just produce a job—it produces the best possible job within the geographical area selected.

YOUR ATTITUDE IS SHOWING*

WHAT IS A POSITIVE ATTITUDE?

On the surface, attitude is the way you communicate your mood or disposition to others. When you are optimistic and anticipate successful encounters, you transmit a positive attitude and others respond favorably. When you are pessimistic and expect the worst, your attitude often is negative and people will tend to classify you as a person they would just as soon avoid. Inside your head, where it all starts, attitude is a mind set. IT IS THE WAY YOU LOOK AT THINGS MENTALLY.

REMEMBER—YOU NEVER
HAVE A SECOND CHANCE
TO MAKE A FIRST
IMPRESSION

---

*For an excellent book on attitude, order *Attitude: Your Most Priceless Possession* from the back of this book.

YOUR ATTITUDE TOWARD THE JOB-FINDING PROCESS

If you don't expect to find the best job available, you probably won't.

To earn a position equal to your potential, it is vital to maintain a positive attitude over an extended period of time. To measure your current attitude toward the job finding process complete this exercise. Circle the appropriate number between the opposite statements. For example, if you circle a 5, you are saying no improvement is possible.

	High				*Low*	
I like searching for prospective employers and setting up interviews.	5	4	3	2	1	I hate having to find a prospective employer.
I love the challenge of an employment interview.	5	4	3	2	1	Interviews bother me.
The prospect of a professional job search excites me.	5	4	3	2	1	I'm depressed before I get started.
An interview can be a dignified experience.	5	4	3	2	1	Interviewing is a demeaning experience.
Going through a dozen interviews to get the best possible job doesn't bother me.	5	4	3	2	1	I hope my first interview is my last.
Selling employers on my talents is fun.	5	4	3	2	1	Having to sell myself is embarrassing.
I want to learn everything I can about the job-finding process.	5	4	3	2	1	I'd rather have someone just offer me a job, or pay an agency.
Interview mistakes can be a positive learning experience.	5	4	3	2	1	Interview mistakes leave me totally discouraged.
Finding a job is a game; I'm going to win!	5	4	3	2	1	Finding a job is like going to the dentist.
I plan to complete three interviews next week.	5	4	3	2	1	I'm taking next week off; job-searching is tiring.

TOTAL SCORE ☐

If you rated yourself above 40, you have an excellent attitude toward the search ahead. If you rated yourself between 25 and 40, you appear to have some adjustments to make. A rating under 25, indicates you are not mentally prepared for your search. Please read on and take this survey again once you have completed this book.

"If you don't want to work you have to work to earn enough money so you won't have to work."

Ogden Nash

CASE #6 | WHO HAS THE ADVANTAGE?

Janet and Christy are equally qualified to seek a position in the same geographical area. Both have open, confident personalities. Both have the same educational background and both are over 30.

The major difference is that Janet already has a job.* She is unhappy because she feels she is underemployed and underpaid, but she likes the steady income and the security. Janet feels her present job constitutes a sound base from which to find a better one. She plans to do her prospecting at night or on weekends. Interviews can be arranged after hours or by taking time off from her present job. Janet has learned that most firms are cooperative in setting interview times for those working. She is convinced she will find a better job than Christy.

Christy is unemployed. Although she has limited savings, she can call on her parents for support during the job-seeking period. Christy feels she has a big advantage over Janet. In the first place, she can devote all of her time to the search and handle up to six interviews per week. She can, also, devote more time to researching organizations, preparing for interviews and working on her wardrobe. Christy feels that searching for and obtaining a position is a full-time endeavor. Best results will come only if one gives the challenge complete and undivided attention. Christy is convinced she will find a better job than Janet.

Which individual, in your opinion, has the advantage? Would you rather search for a job on a full-time basis or while you are employed? Place a check in one of the squares below, write your answer and compare it with that of the author on page 212.

☐ Janet has the advantage because _____

_____

☐ Christy has the advantage because _____

_____

☐ Neither individual has an advantage because _____

_____

———————

*PLAN B (beginning on page 133) is designed to help those in Janet's position.

SELF-CONFIDENCE

A *positive attitude* and *self-confidence* are partners when it comes to searching for and winning the best possible job. It takes self-confidence to arrange an interview and self-confidence to go through a successful interview.

You need not be a fast-talking extrovert to get a good job. Sensitive, quiet people often do better even when the qualifications are the same—providing their inner confidence and positive attitude shine through.

Sometimes it gives your self-confidence a boost when you list your good qualities. If you have trouble doing this, ask a friend to help you. Normally, you project greater confidence to those who know you well than you realize. Please list as many positive characteristics about yourself as you can in the space below.

1.

2.

3.

4.

5.

6.

7.

8.

9.

10.

SELF-CONFIDENCE EXERCISE

You may have rated high in attitude, but if you do not have the confidence to meet those who interview you all is lost. This exercise is designed to help you measure your self-confidence. Read the statements and then circle the number you feel best fits you.

	High				Low
I can convert new co-workers into friends quickly and easily.	5	4	3	2	1
I can attract and hold the attention of others even when I do not know them.	5	4	3	2	1
I enjoy new situations.	5	4	3	2	1
I'm intrigued with the psychology of meeting and building good relationships in a new work environment.	5	4	3	2	1
I know I am capable of doing a good job for a new employer.	5	4	3	2	1
When dressed for the occasion, I have confidence in myself.	5	4	3	2	1
I do not mind using the telephone to make appointments with strangers.	5	4	3	2	1
Large groups do not intimidate me.	5	4	3	2	1
I enjoy solving problems.	5	4	3	2	1
Most of the time, I feel secure.	5	4	3	2	1

TOTAL

If you scored high on both the attitude and self-confidence exercises, you have a winning combination as far as winning a job is concerned. If you scored lower on self-confidence than attitude, you are receiving a signal that you need more experience dealing with people. This program can help increase your self-confidence.

FINDING AND WINNING THE RIGHT JOB MAY BE MORE DIFFICULT THAN WORKING FULL-TIME IN A JOB YOU DON'T LIKE—BUT WITH A POSITIVE ATTITUDE IT CAN BE AN EXCITING CHALLENGE

CASE #7	WHO WILL GET THE BEST JOB?

Wayne and Frank will both graduate from a major university in the spring. Their qualifications are similar and both have confidence in themselves. They are also highly competitive with each other and determined to get the ''better'' first real job.

Wayne is planning a three month search. His strategy calls for a minimum of three interviews each week. He plans to fully prepare for each opportunity. Wayne wants to learn everything he can about each employer ahead of time. His strategy is to spend 75% of his job search time researching and *finding* the best possible prospects. The remaining 25% of his time will be devoted to preparing for and completing the interviews. He expresses his attitude this way: ''It is getting the right kind of interview that concerns me, not the interview itself. I believe I will be hired more on my qualifications than on how I present myself.

Frank plans to devote 25% of his time finding prospects and 75% preparing for and going through interviews. His attitude is expressed this way: ''Look—it is not the quality or even the number of interviews you arrange that makes the difference. You just depend on luck to get good interview opportunities and then use the best possible interview techniques when the time comes. I have already completed two mock interviews to get myself ready. There are many qualified applicants for any available job. The interview makes the difference and that is where I am going to spend my time. All I want are a couple of quality interviews and I will have the best job in my pocket.''

Whom will get the best job? Wayne or Frank?

☐ Wayne will get the best job because _____

_____

☐ Frank will get the best job because _____

_____

Turn to page 212 to compare your answer with that of the author.

Be True to Your Future

PRELIMINARY QUESTIONS

(Write your answers below.)

GEOGRAPHIC AREA IN WHICH I WOULD ACCEPT A JOB WITH ENTHUSIASM: (East Coast? West Coast? Florida? Denver? Home town?)

Few things are worse than living in a geographical area where you (or family members) are unhappy. When it comes to answering this question, be true to yourself and your future.

_____

_____

THREE POSITIONS FOR WHICH I AM PRESENTLY QUALIFIED.

Although it is much better to reach for a job that forces you to live up to your potential than accept one that is beneath your skills, it is still an exercise in futility to apply for a job where the qualifications are so rigid you are not a realistic candidate.

_____

_____

CONSTRAINTS THAT I HAVE? (shift work, length of commute, size of company, etc.)

Some job-seekers accept a position knowing the situation is untenable. When they do this, they are not being true to the prospective employer or their future.

_____

_____

BEGINNING COMPENSATION THAT WOULD BE ACCEPTABLE (Including benefits).

Few events are more disturbing than to accept a job in desperation and then learn later that the job you really wanted was available but you were already working and not in a position to compete for it.

_____

_____

PART 2

PROSPECTING

TO LOCATE EMPLOYERS AND ARRANGE INTERVIEWS, THE SYSTEM YOU USE MAKES THE DIFFERENCE

Like a miner looking for gold, job-seekers must locate employers who need their services and are willing to pay competitive wages. You will probably find you spend more time "prospecting" than you do preparing for and completing job interviews.

As a job hunter, just what is a prospect?

A prospect is an employer with the potential to make you happy as an employee. One where it is worth your time, energy, and commitment to make contact. Not all potential employers are qualified prospects. To be qualified means an employer should be prepared to: (1) make use of your skills (2) provide you with the salary and benefits you require and (3) make you an offer now or in the immediate future.

When it comes to prospecting, most job-seekers make three fundamental mistakes: These are:

Mistake #1: To underestimate the time required and techniques that must be learned. As a result, many wind up accepting jobs beneath their potential. Finding the *right* interview situation is critical.

Mistake #2: Devoting too little time with the search. It is easy to think that preparing for and keeping interviews might take a majority of the time involved to get the best job. Don't believe it! Sometimes the ratio of time spent to get a good interview is five to one. That is, it might take ten hours to get a good interview possibility and only two hours to complete the interview (including transportation).

Mistake #3: Not following a prospecting system. To do a professional job of prospecting requires an organized, consistant approach. A helter-skelter attitude toward prospecting will not normally produce good results.

TRADITIONAL RESOURCES

The first step in professional prospecting is to identify sources for prospective employers who have positions in concert with the life goal(s) you identified on page 10. Employers who will fit your needs as an applicant. Once a source has produced a qualified prospect, you should telephone to verify the information and begin planning to arrange for an "interview" appointment. Below are some of the resources available to most job seekers.

> **NOTE:** A telephone call to a local university or community college will verify if services marked with an * are available.

PRIORITIZE THE LIST BY PLACING A CHECK OPPOSITE THE RESOURCE THAT YOU FEEL WILL PRODUCE THE BEST PROSPECTS FOR YOU. CONTINUE YOUR RANKING UNTIL YOU IDENTIFY THE ONE THAT WILL PRODUCE (IN YOUR OPINION) THE FEWEST OR WEAKEST PROSPECTS. EFFECTIVE JOB-SEARCHERS USE MANY RESOURCES.

☐ **Newspapers.** Classified and help-wanted ads, especially Sunday editions (Some job-seekers attach approropriate ads to their resumes when seeking an interview appointment).

☐ **Campus placement offices.*** Most colleges have placement services and you normally need not be a current student or graduate to participate.

☐ **Internships.** Sometimes volunteer agencies and some operating organizations offer temporary "intern" positions for students (and others). These can be from a few hours per week up to full time for limited periods of time. The intern has an excellent chance to learn more about a given organization or profession. The employer on the other hand has a chance to observe the intern with a possibility of offering a full time position. Internships can also produce an excellent source for letters of recommendation.

☐ **Campus career centers.*** Here you should be able to do serious research on local employers, learn about Civil Service jobs, examination announcements, etc.

☐ **Temporary employment agencies.** Temporary Agencies like Adia, Manpower and Kelly, can provide extra income and potential leads during a job search. They expand opportunities to convert a "temporary" job into a permanent one. You have the added benefit of being able to look over a potential employer carefully.

Be True to Your Future

TRADITIONAL RESOURCES (Continued)

☐ **Networking.** This means to make personal contact with mentors (caring advisors such as teachers, former employers, family members or friends). Anyone who may be able to lead you to a worthwhile interview should be reached through networking (which is discussed in detail in the next section).

☐ **Interviewing for information.** Friends, relatives or co-workers will probably be able to refer you to qualified people who may be willing to discuss the "pros and cons" of the kind of work you are interested in. These "insiders" can often provide prospecting and interviewing tips and sometimes prospecting referrals.

☐ **Private employment agencies.** Normally a fee is involved—but some can be helpful. Check these out carefully before making any commitments.

☐ **Trade magazines dealing with your career area.** Many have Help Wanted ads.

☐ **State Human Resource Offices.** In addition to providing prospects and job-finding seminars, these offices often handle unemployment insurance activities.

☐ **Annual reports.** In these reports, organizations describe their plans for future expansion, new products and services, or shifts in emphasis from past practices. These can be signals to prospect for jobs that will soon open. These reports may be obtained from firms you wish to research by writing to the Public Relations Director at their headquarters, or from your local library.

☐ Public Library. Your public library has a wide variety of resources. Ask the reference librarian to help you.

☐ **OTHERS** (List Your Own):

☐ _____

_____

☐ _____

_____

NETWORKING PRODUCES EXCELLENT LEADS

If you did not place NETWORKING as a top priority on the previous page, you may wish to reconsider. Experts and succesful job-hunters agree that networking, properly understood, constitutes the best job-finding strategy available.

What is networking?

Basically, networking is creating your own employment agency. You do this by cultivating several individuals who may be able to lead you to an excellent prospect. These people (mentors, previous superiors, professionals in your specific career field, etc.) will need to be approached and asked for assistance. Networking should continue indefinitely once it begins.

Some colleges develop ''alumni lists'' composed of names of graduates who are willing to meet with students who are preparing to enter their field. Those who follow-up on these opportunities are adding people to their network at a time when they need it most. Other organizations (such as civic groups) sponsor ''shadow programs'' for persons who desire to enter a specific field or profession. A shadow program allows an interested person to spend some time observing an individual working in a position to which you aspire. Through discussion, observation, and involvement, a job candidate is able to obtain a realistic ''job preview''. Shadow opportunities provide excellent networking contacts.

Those who are already employed can make excellent use of networking because they can use their job to network with others who can offer advice, leads, etc.

Every trade group, professional organization, service club, fraternal society, or club membership is, in effect, an operating network. When you become a member you inherit the network. You still need to make individual contacts but you have a source from which to operate. ''Joiners'' are often network specialists.

To make networking produce, it is vital that mutually rewarding relationships be created with those who can help lead you to prospects. This means that you must gain the respect and support of these key people by providing them with some incentives so they are willing ''to go to bat'' for you.

> Judy, a bank supervisor, decided that she was boxed in with her present firm and needed a fresh start with a larger, more progressive organization. Once each month Judy attended an ABA (American Banking Association) meeting. Judy decided to use her ABA contacts to locate prospects.

(Continued on page 96)

NETWORKING PRODUCES EXCELLENT LEADS (Continued)

Judy: Continued

At the next meeting she met a Francis Able who was in the Human Resource department for a larger bank. During their conversation Francis mentioned she was developing a new employee handbook and was seeking examples from other banks. Judy said she would drop one from her bank in the mail. Then she remembered that her brother worked for a large bank in New York. She called and asked him to send a copy of their employee manual by overnight express. The next day Judy delivered both manuals to Francis and as a result they had lunch together and eventually became close friends. Three months later Francis helped Judy find the job opportunity she had hoped for.

NETWORKING IN ACTION

Met Mrs. Gonzales at Trade Fair June 7. She suggested I contact Mr. Kern at Trim Tech

June 11
Took Mr. Kern to lunch. Discovered we had much in common. He made an appointment to see a John Grant at Jaco Co.

June 18
Mr. Grant, a Vice President took me to their Human Resource Director. Two interviews followed

June 30
Accepted position with Jaco

MY PERSONAL NETWORKING SYSTEM
(One contact leads to another)

Please use this page to list those special individuals who are *already* part of your networking system. To be on your list you should feel comfortable calling them to guide you to prospective employers. Once these people are listed (*please* include telephone numbers) you are ready to add new members to your network. Do not add a name until you have built a potentially mutually rewarding relationship. PLEASE KEEP IN MIND THAT ANYONE ON THIS LIST CAN LEAD YOU TO ANOTHER, WHO MAY IN TURN, LEAD YOU TO ANOTHER, WHO WILL OFFER YOU THE JOB YOU SEEK.

_____

_____

_____

_____

_____

_____

A systematic way to implement this program would be to start a 3×5 Card Index File with contact names and telephone numbers, along with other information such as comments about who referred you and the field they represent.

DOING A NUMBER ON THE TELEPHONE

Making employment interview appointments by phone saves time, transportation costs and is professionally accepted. This exercise will help prepare you to do this more effectively. With your completed PROSPECT LIST in front of you, take the following steps:

Step 1: Dial Number.

Step 2: While waiting for an answer put a smile in your voice. (Actually smile so your voice will have a friendly tone.)

Step 3: If you do not have a personal contact, when someone answers, ask to speak with the personnel office (for a large company) or the employer (in a small company). Say: "I'm seeking an employment interview and would appreciate your help."

Step 4: When party answers, give your full name and say: "I would like to arrange for an interview for the position of _____." If answering an advertisement for a specific position, mention the publication and the exact title.

Step 5: Communicate an upbeat, positive attitude. Whatever arrangements may or may not be made, be sure to thank the individual *by name* for the help you have received.

Step 6: Ask your contact for advice about any other steps you could/should take.

Step 7: Record date, time and location of any appointments. Be sure you have the name of the person you spoke to and clear directions on how to find the interview site.

PLACE A CHECK IN THE SQUARE IF YOU AGREE WITH THE FOLLOWING SUGGESTIONS.

☐ 1. Try to cluster your calls.

☐ 2. Group your appointments. If you make a morning appointment some distance from your home, try for an afternoon appointment near your first interview.

☐ 3. Do not accept appointments unless the job sounds promising.

☐ 4. Always ask for directions and draw a map before you leave home.

CASE #8	WHICH PROSPECTING SYSTEM IS BEST?

Mary and Jessie view prospecting for job interviews differently.

Mary intends to spend Monday and Tuesday of each week prospecting and Wednesday and Thursday for interview appointments. Her rationale is: "I can stay at home in casual clothes Monday and Tuesday as I do my telephoning or check out resources in the community. Then, on Wednesday and Thursday, I will gear up for interviews. When Thursday evening arrives I'll relax and get ready for the next Monday. Friday and Monday are not good days for interviews. I think this is a system that will work for me."

Jessie has a less structured strategy. He plans to do his prospecting in the morning and try to get at least one interview each afternoon. Jessie will take an interview when he can get it. His rationale is: "Flexibility is the key. It is always possible to make a call and have the person in charge suggest an immediate interview. In other cases, I might need a full day to prepare for a priority interview. I'm going to work in both directions—prospecting and interviewing at the same time. I think my system will produce more interviews and I will handle them better."

Which prospecting system would be best for you?

Which system would produce the best results?

Please place a check in the appropriate square and compare your answers with those of the author on page 212.

☐ Mary's plan would be best for me because _____

_____

☐ I like Jessie's plan best because _____

_____

CREATIVE RESUMES, USED PROPERLY, PRODUCE PROSPECTS. TWO LEADING BOOKS IN THIS AREA ARE:

1. *High Impact Resumes & Letters**
   Ron Kramich
   Impact Publications
   Manassas, VA 22111
   $12.95

2. *Designing Creative Resumes**
   Gregg Berryman
   William Kaufmann, Inc.,
   Los Altos, California.
   $14.95

Check your library or career center for others.

---

*Available through Crisp Publications, 95 First Street, Los Altos, CA 94022.

THE RESUME AS A SUPPORT DOCUMENT

To do an effective job search, you will need copies of a professional-looking resume to give contacts. A resume is a one or two page summary of your previous employment experience and education. It is a supplemental form of communication designed to give a prospective employer a quick reveiw of your history and potential. The purpose of a resume is to win you an interview or support you during an interview. Resumes may either be mailed (along with a personal letter), attached to application forms in an employer's office, or best of all presented during or following an interview.

Some basic tips:

- A resume should show your best side and make a prospective employer want to see you in person.

- It should contain information relevant to the job you are seeking.

- The information must be honest.

- The more sophisticated the job, the more effective your resume should be.

- Always have someone (such as a counselor in a placement or career center), critique your draft, and make suggestions for improvement.

- Writing a resume should help you organize your thoughts prior to an interview.

- Resumes should be individually typed or professionally reproduced.

- Resumes must be letter-perfect when it comes to spelling and grammar.

- Developing a professional resume takes time. Most job-seekers go through 3 or 4 drafts before they are satisfied with the organization and content of their resume.

- Be sure to include your ''job objective'' at the beginning of the resume. Highlight all relevant activities and experiences that support your objective.

> **If a resume isn't done right,**
> **it shouldn't be done at all!**

SAMPLE RESUMES →

SAMPLE RESUME—LIMITED EXPERIENCE

ROBERTA J. ADAMS
400 Westview Way #211
Marvin Gardens, California
(408) 633-6789

OBJECTIVE   To obtain a challenging teaching position in Language Arts for Junior High School or High School

EDUCATION   California Teaching Certificate—September 19XX
(128 Practice Teaching Hours)

California State Polytechnic University, Pomona
M.A. English—June 19XX (GPA 3.87)

California State Polytechnic University, Pomona
B.S. (with Honors)—December 19XX

EXPERIENCE

August 1987 to present   **Graduate Assistant**—California Polytechnic, Pomona
Responsible for teaching classes within the English Developmental Program (EDP).

March 1986 August 1987   **Lead English Tutor**—California Polytechnic, Pomona
Responsible for training all new tutors in Cal Poly English Development Program. Also served as primary liaison between Cal Poly English Department and the Educational Opportunity Program (EOP).

August 1984 March 1986   **Counselor**—Christian Fellowship Society, First Church, Pomona
Responsible for conducting small group counseling meetings as well as serving as one-on-one counselor for persons requesting individualized attention.

ACTIVITIES & ACHIEVEMENTS   Academic Honor's List—(9 straight semesters)
Cal Poly Field Hockey Team (3 years)
Lauren Hall Student Government Representative

REFERENCES   Dr. John P. Harris, Head
English Department, California Polytechnic University, Pomona

Dr. Stephen B. Kellock, Director
California Polytechnic University Student Teaching

Ms. Susan P. Dibble, Director
First Church Christian Fellowship Society, Pomona

SAMPLE RESUME—LIMITED EXPERIENCE

Jon C. Kies   January 19XX
440 Peralta Ave
Long Beach, Ca. 90803
(213) 430-0221

OBJECTIVES   **Trainee Position in Finance/Accounting Leading to Higher
Management Levels**

SKILLS/   Leadership (See below)   Group Interaction
TRAITS   Spreadsheet Creation   Learning Attitude
                   Lotus 123, DOS, Wordstar   Self-Motivated

EDUCATION   California State University Long Beach
                   B.S. Degree-Business Administration Dec. 19XX
                   Major: **Finance** Upper Division Core GPA: **3.65**
                   Deans List Spring, Fall 19XX

                   University of California, Berkley   19XX-XX
                        Area of Study: Social Science

                   Long Beach City College   19XX-XX
                        Area of Study: Business and General Education
                        Deans List Fall 19XX
                        Water Polo Team Captain, Metro League Champions

**WORK
EXPERIENCE**
May, 19XX   Seal Beach Lifeguard Department
Present   *Position:* **Lifeguard Supervisor**
                   Responsibilities:
                        Public Safety via Lifesaving, First Aid.
                        Supervision of 4-8 Lifeguards.
                        On Duty Training of Lifeguards.
                   Accomplishments:
                        Negotiated M.O.U. for Seasonal Lifeguards.
                        Developed Employee Evaluation Profile.
                        Tower Lifeguard of Year 19XX.

Aug., 19XX   Bobby McGee's Conglemeration Long Beach, CA.
Apr., 19XX   Restaurant and Bar
                   Position: **Door Host (Department Head), Bartender**
                   Responsibilities:
                        Greet, Assist, and Interface with Guests
                        Interview, Hire, an Train Door Hosts
                        Manage and Schedule 6-8 Door Hosts
                   Accomplishments:
                        Employee of the Month October 19XX
                        Promoted to Department Coordinator

INTERESTS   Skiing, SCUBA, basketball, reading.

REFERENCES   Available upon Request

SAMPLE RESUME—EXTENSIVE EXPERIENCE

A. Lee Cramer 1101 32nd Avenue, Seal Beach, California 90740

B. (714) 329-6391
H. (714) 430-5566

OBJECTIVE   **EXECUTIVE MANAGEMENT/COMMUNICATIONS - Graphics**

SUMMARY   16 years of managerial experience in typesetting. Highly skilled in administration and scheduling in all aspects of pre-press graphics. Intimate knowledge of printing operations of magazines, books and newsletters. Work well in pressure situations. Fully support clients through production phase of projects. Excellent sales generator.

EXPERIENCE
19XX to
Present

Currently Marketing Director with **Dunn Bros. Printers, Inc.** and their affiliates— *Digital Typographers, Inc.* and *Golden West Bindery, Inc.*

- Established Marketing Program as follows:

  — Creation of promotional kit describing history, services and equipment of organization. This involved copy writing, design, photography and total execution of project.

  — Graphic display booth utilized at trade shows.

  — Creation of new client contact data base.

19XX thru
19XX

BENWAY, MAXWELL & SMITH, INC., Chatham, New Jersey
President

- In 19XX, expanded services to include copy telecommunications from word processing/computers directly into Compugraphic system.

  — Created procedure for transmittal of typeset galleys to clients within 4 hours for proofreading and alterations.

  — Set up disc file storage system to maintain documentation on file for future revisions by clients.

  — Reduced clients' costs by editing transmitted copy in lieu of re-keyboarding documents from hard manuscript editorial.

  — Reduced cumulative pre-press production and printing time from 7 days to 4 days.

  — Originated and administered a support system to clients by working directly with printing companies through each printing function, i.e. supervision of stripping, blueprinting, platemaking and conducting press checks.

- 19XX, relocated firm to new and larger quarters. Updated equipment to fit technological advances in the graphics field.

  — Managed entire relocation project. Worked with architectural firm to create the space for proper work flow.

  — Researched manufacturers and vendors to acquire proper equipment, necessary furnishings and tools to ensure efficient production capabilities.

- From 19XX to 19XX, established typesetting organization, created a client list, generated sales and opened offices in Madison, NJ. Worked with top management in the hiring of appropriate personnel and acquiring equipment.

19XX to
19XX

DAVID T. HOUSTON CO. (Industrial Real Estate Broker)
Bloomfield, New Jersey

Manager

- Coordinated and administered field support for 16 sales personnel.

- Organized direct mail and newspaper advertising programs for sales staff.

19XX to
19XX

DIAMOND SHAMROCK CO., Morristown, New Jersey

Services Manager

- Managed and directed duplicating services personnel.

- Directed and administered the scheduling of all inter-office duplicating services.

- Coordinated the distribution of all company mail - internal and external.

19XX to
19XX

ROGERS, SLADE & HILL, INC. (Management Consultants)
30 Madison Avenue, New York, N.Y.

Report Department and Office Service Supervisor

- Supervised Report Department responsible for printing, graphics and consultant report typing services.

- Worked with consultants in the graphic reproduction of client reports.

- Coordinated the relocation of firm from its Fifth Avenue offices to the Madison Avenue location.

EDUCATION

Chatham High School, Chatham, New Jersey
School of Visual Arts, New York City, N.Y.
Hunter College, New York City, N.Y.-Supervisory courses
Rutgers University, Newark, N.J.-Accounting and Supervisory Practices

MILITARY

U.S. Naval Reserve (3 years inactive - 2 years active)

PERSONAL

Married, 3 children

REFERENCES

Furnished upon request.

IMPORTANT: Notice the extensive use of ''action'' words in the narrative that show achievement, creativity, and problem-solving abilities on the job-seekers part. All of these specifics are eagerly saught by progressive employers. Can you pick out several ''action'' words that could be added to your own resume?

SAMPLE COVER LETTER

Sometimes the cover letter which is sent with your resume is as important as the resume itself. Effective job-seekers usually "customize" cover letters to fit the job being sought.

June 16, 19XX

Mr. James W. Roman
Vice President, Marketing
Sports World, Inc.
Tower Square
Los Angeles, CA 91122

Dear Mr. Roman,

   Your advertisement in this week's *Los Angeles Examiner* for a sales representative caught my attention. I have a strong interest in both sports and selling, and have been impressed by your firm's reputation of providing quality sports equipment.

   Last month I graduated from Chaffey College with an A.A. degree in Marketing Management. My GPA was 3.1 (out of a possible 4.0). As a student, I completed a class project dealing with marketing sporting goods to a new generation of consumers. The enclosed resume will provide a summary of my qualifications.

   I would like to discuss the possibility of joining your staff as a sales trainee. I will call you next week to learn if an appointment can be arranged.

Sincerely yours,

Rebecca Alaras
1604 South Hood
Claremont, CA 91729

IMPORTANT: See a Placement Office, Career Center, or Library for other resume formats. Another model may be more appropriate for your needs.

THE RIGHT FOLLOW-UP LETTER CAN MAKE A GOOD IMPRESSION AND TURN UP A NEW LEAD

Once an interview has taken place (whether or not a job offer has been made) a follow-up letter might improve your chances and lead to other, more productive interviews. For example, an acceptance letter will help you get off on the right foot with an organization. A job inquiry letter may produce a prospect. Following are six letters that fit various job-hunting situations. You may wish to use them as models.

ACCEPTANCE LETTER

Your address
Telephone #

Name, title, address
of organization

Dear Ms. Smith:

Thank you for your confidence in offering me the position of Administrative Assistant with your firm. According to your letter I will report directly to Mr. Jay, Training Director, on Monday, June 5.

The salary is acceptable and I am pleased with the six-month review in which my progress will be evaluated. Your offer of immediate full medical/dental insurance is excellent.

I am grateful for the opportunity and know you will not be disappointed. If you or members of your staff need to contact me before I begin work, please call me at the number above.

Sincerely,

Karen Henderson

REQUEST FOR DELAY

Your address
Telephone #

Name, title, address
of organization

Dear Mr. Campbell:

Thank you for the job offer letter which I received yesterday. I consider the offer attractive and am giving it serious consideration.

You requested an acceptance or refusal of the offer by July 15th. I would greatly appreciate an extension to July 30 in order to make a certain decision. I will call to learn if you are able to arrange this extension.

Thank you for your considerations.

Sincerely,

Jane Draper

INTERVIEW FOLLOW-UP LETTER

Your address
Telephone #

Name, position, address
of organization

Dear Mr. Hill:

Thank you for the interview last Monday. I extended your greetings to
Professor James when I returned to campus.

The tour of your facility was appreciated and I am more excited than ever
about the possibility of joining your firm.

If you need additional information please feel free to contact me
otherwise, I will follow up as we agreed the week of the fifteenth.

Sincerely,

Jack Smith

REJECTING A JOB OFFER

Your address
Telephone #

Name, position, address
of organization

Dear Ms. Harris:

Thank you for the job offer and the time you spent with me during the
interview process. As I mentioned following our meeting, the position
offered is not right for me. It was a hard decision for me to make but one
which I believe is correct.

I appreciate your interest and wish you success in making an excellent
hiring choice.

Sincerely,

Kay Right

REJECTION FOLLOW-UP LETTER

Your address
Telephone #

Name, title, address
of organization

Dear Mr. Crane:

Naturally I was disappointed not to be offered the Senior Engineer
position. I appreciate, however, your candor in explaining the reason for
the decision. Following your suggestion, I will start making my position
stronger for future possibilities.

Please keep me in mind for any other opportunities which are appropriate
for my qualifications. I hope to contact you at a later date.

Sincerely,

Gregg Smith

JOB INQUIRY LETTER

Your address
Telephone #

Name, title, address
of organization

Dear Ms. Armstrong:

Mr. Fred Grace, Director of Human Resources with the DEMK
Corporation, suggested I contact you. He informed me that you may be
seeking a marketing person with supermarket and food-processing
experience.

Enclosed is my resume.

I would welcome an opportunity to discuss my qualifications and will call
you next Monday at 10:00 am to see if an interview can be arranged.

Sincerely,

Ricardo Torres

| CASE #9 | WHICH STRATEGY IS SUPERIOR? |

Jake and Rose have been given notice by their firm (bankruptcy is pending) and they are in the process of preparing their best possible resume, but have different views about how they are to be used.

At considerable cost, Jake plans to have 500 resumes and cover letter printed and send them to every firm he can locate in the area. With this broadside approach, Jake expects to receive 25 replies—enough in his estimation to lead him to the best opportunity available. Jake's attitude regarding resumes is as follows: "I want to win the best possible job in the shortest amount of time. I intend to prepare three resumes, have a placement counselor help me select the best of the three and then do a mass mailing. This should provide all of the interviews I need to find the right opportunity. I have faith in resumes They are the best way to market myself effectively."

Rose has a different strategy. She intends to perfect her resume in the same manner as Jake, but will have 25 copies professionally typed and send them to a select group of prospects. Rose feels she will have to produce two interviews through her personal networking efforts for every interview that sending a resume will uncover. Rose will take a resume with her for each interview, but does not place much faith in resumes leading to interviews. Rose's attitude is: "Applicants overestimate the value of resumes. Networking and using the telephone produce better results."

Which strategy do you feel will bring the best results?

☐ Jake has the best marketing plan because _____

_____

☐ Rose has the best marketing plan because _____

_____

To compare your views with those of the author, please turn to page 212.

LIVE PROSPECTS
(WORTH AN INTERVIEW)

An organized prospecting system (featuring networking) should provide a job-seeker with a *continuous* list of promising interviews. For a person job hunting on a full-time basis, the system (fully operational) should normally produce two or three legitimate prospects per week. Remember, a legitimate prospect is one worthy of an interview and interviews require time, transportation and energy.

To get started, you may wish to list a few prospects in the spaces below *now*. When time permits (after completing this program) you will be adding new prospects on a continuous basis. Securing a promising interview is not a signal to stop prospecting. If the interview does not produce a job you have wasted valuable time.

PROSPECTIVE EMPLOYER	NAME OF CONTACT	TELEPHONE

PROSPECTING LIST

PROSPECTIVE EMPLOYER	NAME OF CONTACT	TELEPHONE

Make copies of this sheet for easier use. Keep your prospect list active until you win the job your way!

SCHEDULING INTERVIEW APPOINTMENTS*

During any job-hunting period it is essential to keep a schedule of interview appointments in front of you at all times. As you set up your appointments, you may wish to keep the following suggestions in mind:

(1) Depending upon how much transportation is involved, most people believe that not more than two interviews should be scheduled on any day.

(2) Do not schedule an interview unless you are sure you have a qualified prospect and would be enthusiastic about accepting the right job should it be offered.

(3) Many placement counselors feel that interview appointments should not be scheduled over two weeks in advance.

		MONDAY	TUESDAY	WEDNESDAY	THURSDAY	FRIDAY
Week 1	AM					
	PM					
Week 2	AM					
	PM					
Week 3	AM					
	PM					
Week 4	AM					
	PM					
Week 5	AM					
	PM					
Week 6	AM					
	PM					

*You may wish to replace this with a larger calendar or a Week-At-A-Glance notebook of your choosing.

PART 3

THE INTERVIEW PROCESS

INTERVIEW STRATEGY

Conducting a successful employment interview can be compared to playing baseball. Similar strategies and techniques are involved, but you need not be a baseball fan to make them work. Consider the following.

(1) Just like a baseball player taking a turn at bat, most job-seekers are nervous before an interview. This is natural and to be expected. Being nervous can actually help an applicant do better.

(2) The more you know about the pitcher (prospective employer) the better prepared you will be to handle any curves. To prepare for an interview, it is wise to learn as much as possible about the organization in advance (talk to employees, read brochures and other literature, etc.). Good preparation can do wonders for your batting average.

(3) In baseball nothing really happens until you score a run. It is the same with a job search. All of your prospecting efforts lead toward the best possible job offer. When an acceptable offer is made, you have won the game.

(4) As you approach each interview you need a GAME PLAN. The pages ahead will give you such a plan. The four step strategy presented will not only give you more personal confidence, it will make you more effective.

JOB SEARCH MYTHS

1. **The longer you are out of a job the harder you try to get one.**
2. **It is easier to get a job in a small firm than a large one.**
3. **It is easy to hide your real attitude during the interviewing process.**

GET AROUND THE BASES AND YOU WIN THE JOB

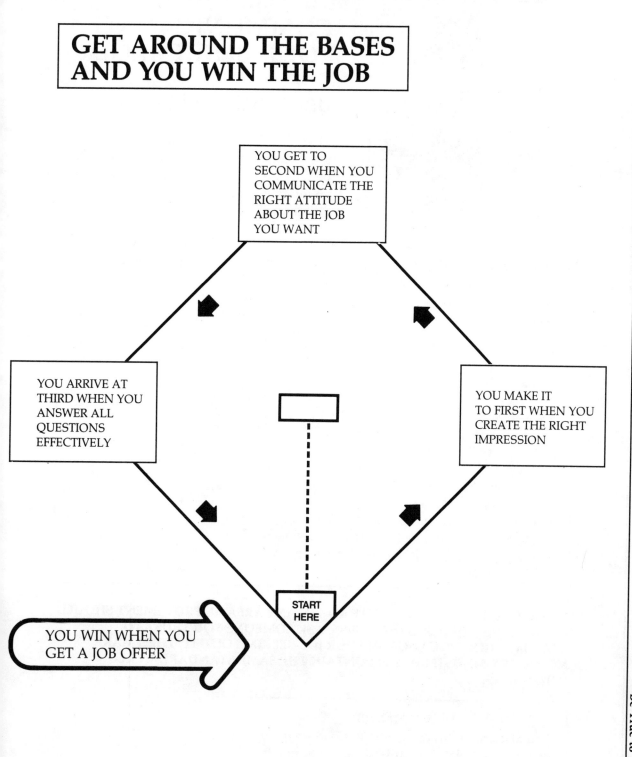

YOU GET TO
SECOND WHEN YOU
COMMUNICATE THE
RIGHT ATTITUDE
ABOUT THE JOB
YOU WANT

YOU ARRIVE AT
THIRD WHEN YOU
ANSWER ALL
QUESTIONS
EFFECTIVELY

YOU MAKE IT
TO FIRST WHEN YOU
CREATE THE RIGHT
IMPRESSION

START
HERE

YOU WIN WHEN YOU
GET A JOB OFFER

COMMUNICATING YOUR BEST IMAGE

DRESS FOR SUCCESS!

There is a direct connection between your appearance and your self-confidence. The better your self-image when you arrive for an interview, the more positive your attitude will be.

To help you prepare, some specific grooming areas are presented below. Combined they constitute the physical image you will communicate. Rate yourself in each area by circling the appropriate number. A **5** indicates no further improvement is possible. A **3** or lower indicates improvement is needed. BE HONEST! Most job-seekers have difficulty seeing improvements that can be made.

	High				Low
1. Hairstyle, hair grooming (neat/clean)	5	4	3	2	1
2. Personal hygiene (clean fingernails, etc.)	5	4	3	2	1
3. Cleanliness of clothing (pressed?)	5	4	3	2	1
4. Appropriate shoes (clean, polished?)	5	4	3	2	1
5. Choice of clothing (conservative?)	5	4	3	2	1
6. Choice of clothing (Appropriate for the work environment you seek?)	5	4	3	2	1
7. Accessories (not too wild)	5	4	3	2	1
8. *General statement:* Once you are ready for an interview and you look in the mirror, you make a statement. Is it what you really want to look like?	5	4	3	2	1

IF YOU RATED YOURSELF LESS THAN 3 IN ANY AREA, IMPROVEMENT SHOULD BE YOUR FIRST ORDER OF BUSINESS. ASK SOMEONE YOU TRUST TO EVALUATE HOW YOU LOOK IN YOUR JOB-SEEKING OUTFIT, THEN MAKE NECESSARY ADJUSTMENTS. MAINTAIN THE SAME STANDARD IN ALL INTERVIEWS.

REMINDER
You also, communicate a good or bad image by the way you complete an application. Print neatly—answer all questions—use words you know how to spell correctly.

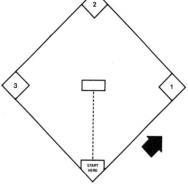

STEP 1
HOW TO GET
TO FIRST BASE

If you don't send the right signals to the person who
has the authority to hire you, the game is over before
you get started. Here are four tips that should help you.

1. **Send non-verbal signals first.** A non-verbal signal is a smile,
   your posture, the way you dress, your walk and other body
   signals. Eye-contact is an important signal to transmit early.
   When entering an office for an interview, demonstrate you are
   confident and energetic by sending positive non-verbal signals
   before you say anything.

2. **Use a verbal greeting that is natural.** Say something like:
   ''I'm Kathy. Thanks for seeing me.'' Or: ''I'm Joe Hicks. It is a
   pleasure to meet you.'' Let the interviewer know you are
   comfortable with yourself. Shake hands firmly.

3. **Once seated, show a reserved confidence.** Let the interviewer
   start the dialogue. Remember the interviewer wants to know
   more about you. You, in turn want to know more about the
   job. At the start it is a good idea to listen until you are
   prompted to talk. Have a few good questions prepared *before*
   the interview.

4. **Discover if the job is for you.** There is no need to go around
   the bases if you know you don't want the job. Once you
   realize you are not interested, say so in a friendly way. It is
   appropriate to ask if there will be an opening for a position you
   are interested in now or in the future.

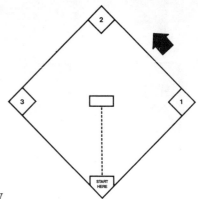

STEP 2
IT IS NOT ALWAYS EASY
TO GET TO SECOND BASE

Once you are securely on first base (i.e. your interview is off to a good start), the person conducting the interview will be evaluating your attitude as you answer and ask questions. MAKE SURE YOU COMMUNICATE THE FOLLOWING ATTITUDES:

Attitude #1: You are willing to work. The key word in any organization is productivity. It is not so much your education and experience, but whether or not you can get your productivity to a high level quickly. One way to communicate this is to emphasize that you do not mind working hard. It is always a good idea to provide some examples from your past.

Attitude #2: You are anxious to learn. Some applicants make the mistake of communicating the attitude that they already know all the answers. A better attitude is to say: "What I don't know I will be anxious to learn." You can transmit a good *learning attitude* by asking intelligent questions which indicate a willingness to learn.

Attitude #3: You are flexible. One thing you do not want to communicate is that you may be a problem employee. Employers want employees who can adjust, work well with others and fit into a new environment without complaints or special requests. If you honestly believe you are flexible and have good human relations, you should make it known during the interview. Again, illustrate these convictions with personal situations where you have been successful in the past.

Attitude #4: You expect to make a contribution. If an interviewer thinks you will make the organization stronger by your creativity, productivity and problem-solving contributions, you should make it to second base with ease.

**YOUR ATTITUDE OFTENS SPEAKS LOUDER
THAN ANYTHING YOU SAY**

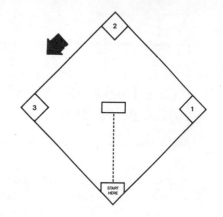

STEP 3
INTERVIEWERS CAN
THROW CURVES

Sometimes, those who are responsible for hiring employees ask difficult questions to learn how the interviewee will cope. For example, what if these questions were asked of you?

"Why do you want to work here?"
"What can you contribute?"
"Why should we hire you?"
"Why did you leave your last job?"
"What are your weaknesses?"

How you answer and handle uncomfortable questions like these will, in large measure, determine whether you get to third base. Anticipating questions similar to the above and role playing your answers with a friend (or in front of a mirror) is helpful. Practicing is a key to effective job interviewing preparation. Here are some tips.

Welcome all questions with a smile. The moment you show irritation can be the moment you will be out of the competition. You can say: "That's a good question. I believe I have a good answer." The manner in which you answer questions is often as important as the answer you provide.

Give direct, honest answers. You need not rush your answers, but try not to be indecisive. Indirect or awkward answers can cast a cloud over your credibility. Be straightforward. An honest answer, even if not perfect, will send a better signal than one that is wishy-washy.

Ask questions in return. It is a good idea to go into each interview with prepared questions you want answered. An example might be:

"When I do a good job, what opportunities will I have for additional experience?"

A potential employer has the right to reject you as an employee during your interview. You, also, have the right to withdraw from an interview if you are not satisfied with the answers you receive.

Introduce the mutual reward idea. When the time is appropriate, indicate you understand that an ideal situation is when both the employer and employee benefit. You can get to third base by discussing what you can do for the firm and asking directly what the organization can do for you.

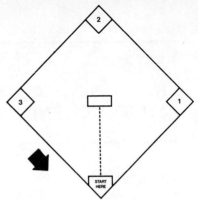

STEP 4
THE LAST MOVE MAY
BE UP TO YOU

Many teams could have made it to the World Series if they had not stranded so many players on third base. Many applicants could have won a desired position if they had displayed appropriate levels of interest and confidence. Here are some ideas to help you get home safely, and win the job you want.

Demonstrate your interest by asking when the position will be filled. This question will often reveal whether you are in the running and when a decision can be expected. You are, in effect, taking the initiative.

During the later stages of the interview, introduce a discussion on financial arrangements. You have a right to know the starting salary and whether or not it is negotiable. Also, what benefits are included. You may wish to learn other factors such as special shift pay, etc. If the discussion convinces you the arrangements are satisfactory, say so. You could say: ''The financial conditions you describe are fair and would be acceptable. If not, tactfully state: ''I believe we have several areas of agreement, with the exception of salary.''

Summarize why you feel qualified. Do this in a few well-chosen sentences such as: ''The more you describe the job and your organization, the more enthusiastic I become. I believe my qualifications have prepared me for the demands of the job, and I would make a positive contribution in the area of customer relations and account maintenance.''

If you want the job, say so. The following expressions show an attitude that employers would react to in a positive manner:

''I am genuinely interested in the job.''

''It seems like a great opportunity. I hope I'm selected.''

DON'T OVERSTAY YOUR TIME

It is a mistake to drag an interview beyond a reasonable point. When you sense you have done your best to cover all four bases, stand up, smile, shake hands, and exit with confidence. A positive departure might be just the action that will turn the decision in your favor.

EVERY INTERVIEW CAN BE A GROWTH EXPERIENCE. DON'T FEEL SORRY FOR SOMEONE WHO GOES THROUGH TEN OR MORE TO FIND THE RIGHT JOB.

A MOCK INTERVIEW IS A LITTLE LIKE TAKING A SCREEN TEST FOR A MOVIE

IT IS POSSIBLE TO ENJOY AND LEARN FROM THE EXPERIENCE

PRACTICE BUILDS CONFIDENCE

(This exercise is primarily for those who have had little experience with the interview process or those who have been away from it a long time.)

Perhaps the best way to demonstrate you are ready for your first interview is to do a dry run or "mock" interview. One way to do this is to have a friend or relative play the role of the employer while you play the role of the applicant. A third person can play the role of silent observer, who provides feedback to both the "employer" and "job-candidate" about the interview. Consider videotaping the process if possible to observe your efforts later.

The first thing to do is review the four steps in the previous baseball analogy. Make sure that all involved in the interview cover all four bases, (especially getting from second to third many questions need to be asked). Try to make the mock interview last at least fifteen minutes.

The next thing to do is to give the person playing the employer the information listed in the left hand column to study. While she or he is doing this, study the information in the right hand column. When you both feel comfortable with the material, start the practice interview and play the roles assigned. That is, be Mr. Grimm (employer) and Ms. Competence (applicant).

THE ROLE OF MS./MR. GRIMM

You are a professional interviewer for a large technical firm. You are seeking a secretary for a demanding Vice President and you want to make sure the applicant you select can handle the job. Your technique is to be polite, but ask difficult questions. You have interviewed six people for the job starting at 9:00 o'clock this morning. None have been satisfactory. You have just offered Ms. Competence a chair and said: "Please tell me about yourself."

THE ROLE OF MS./MR. COMPETENCE

You are an experienced secretary with all the necessary skills. You are nervous however, because you have never worked for a large technical firm and the salary is well above any you have received in the past. You have, however, gone over the four points in the baseball analogy and intend to put them into practice. Mr. Grimm has just asked you to be seated and has asked you the question "Tell me about yourself."

POST INTERVIEW LET DOWNS

It is natural to encounter a letdown feeling after an interview (even a good one). The truth is that most people do better with interviews than they think. It is not uncommon for an applicant to say he or she ''blew'' an interview and then get the job.

In any situation, it is difficult to say things perfectly. Sometimes applicants come on too strong and leave the wrong impression. Sometimes those interviewed understate their case. Perfect balance is hard to achieve.

Once an interview is over, the most important thing you can do is learn from it and build a positive attitude for your next interview opportunity. Make some notes on how you did. It may help to ask yourself these questions:

Did I oversell? If you paint too perfect an image, you may raise a question about your objectivity. It is surprising how many applicants talk themselves out of a job.

Did I communicate excessive interest in my career? If you place your own interests too far ahead of the organization, you might be considered a poor risk.

Did I infer I would be underemployed? Many highly-educated people communicate (often without knowing it) that they would be bored with a starting job and, therefore, not produce as much as someone less qualified. This could be a signal to pass you up.

Did I mention my human relation skills? Keep in mind that organizations are seeking good team players, who can compromise and build healthy relationships with others.

Did I communicate dependability? It helps if you can convince the interviewer that you believe in meeting commitments.

Did I say enough about productivity? It is a good idea to demonstrate pride in your ability to live up to your potential. An example might be: ''My goal during my senior year was to make the honor roll, and I did it!''

> IT IS NOT WHAT HAPPENED AT THE LAST INTERVIEW BUT WHAT HAPPENS AT THE NEXT ONE THAT IS IMPORTANT.

PART 4

HANG IN THERE!

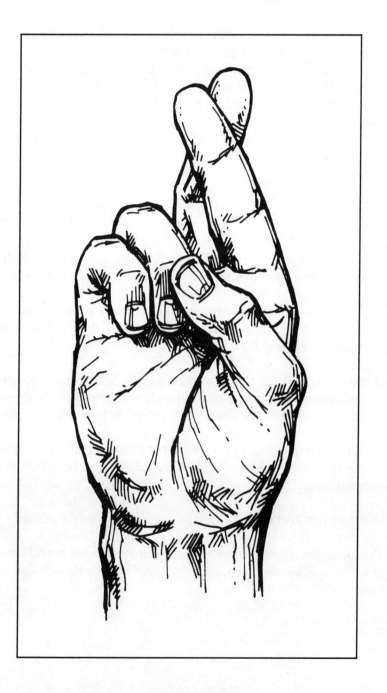

HOW TO STAY POSITIVE DURING A LONGER THAN ANTICIPATED JOB SEARCH

One can never tell in advance just how long a job search may take. Market conditions, job availability for the position you want, and "being at the right place at the right time" all have an important part to play in the experience. It is vital during this period that you do not settle for a permanent job that is substantially beneath your potential or in conflict with your life goal. Rather than do this, it is better to take a lower-paying temporary job that will "pay the bills" while you continue your search for the job you really want.

SUGGESTIONS:

- A "healthy appearance" is a major factor during a job search. If you are not already in an exercise program; begin one. Exercise will not only help you look fit during an interview—it will help you remain positive about yourself.

- Set weekly interview goals in advance. Two per week should be a minimum if you are unemployed. Five interviews is often a reachable goal. When you reach a goal give yourself a reward.

- You need the help of others to pull you back up when you are down. This can be a friend, advisor, or relative. Keep in touch with these support people—make sure the Mutual Reward Theory is working between you and them.

- If you find it necessary to back away from your search, take a complete break so you can come back refreshed and with vigor. Make sure however that your break is not too long.

- Believe in the power and effectiveness of your own positive attitude.

- Review this program frequently to rekindle your motivation and refresh your techniques. Pay special attention to the material that deals with life goals. Be true to your future.

CASE #10 — WHO WILL REMAIN POSITIVE THE LONGEST?

Grace and Sam lost similar positions with the same company when it was acquired by a competitor. Each is eligible for unemployment insurance during their search for a new position.

Having gone through a difficult job search three years ago, Grace knows her chances are good only so long as she can remain positive during her search. Here are things Grace intends to do to maintain her positive attitude until she finds the best possible job.

1. Spend increased time on grooming and fitness to improve her image and attitude.
2. Give herself a special reward each time she completes an interview.
3. Limit interviews to two days each week so as not to burn out too soon.
4. Read some "motivational" books.
5. Spend some time thinking about the life goals she previously listed.

Sam is, also, realistic about what lies ahead. He intends to remain positive by doing the following during his search period.

1. Maintain a daily exercise program—not less than one hour at his health club.
2. Spend four days each week looking for prospects and keeping interview appointments.
3. Prepare an action plan for each day ahead of time.
4. Maintain a good social life, talking with friends, seeking support, asking advice.
5. Spend time discussing life goals with close friends.

Which plan, in your opinion, will do the most to keep Grace or Sam positive during their search?

☐ I think Grace has the best plan because _____

_____

☐ I believe that Sam has a superior plan because _____

_____

To compare your views with those of the author on page 213.

"Nothing is really work unless you would rather be doing something else."

James M. Barrie

SELF-TEST

This book has presented a job finding *system*. To test yourself on how much you have learned please answer the following true and false questions.

True   **False**

_____   _____   1. Prospecting and interviewing are considered as separate functions but can be performed on the same day.

_____   _____   2. Prospecting is not demanding and consumes a small amount of time for the average job-seeker.

_____   _____   3. Traditional resources should not be ignored in favor of networking.

_____   _____   4. Networking is like creating your own employment agency.

_____   _____   5. A resume is both a prospecting technique *and* a support document to take on interview appointments.

_____   _____   6. A qualified (live) prospect is one that is worthy of an interview, if it can be arranged.

_____   _____   7. Going around the bases (baseball analogy) is designed to improve one's prospecting strategy.

_____   _____   8. The baseball comparison can help you know at what stage you are in the interview process; thus you can react in a more professional manner.

_____   _____   9. A mock interview can help you work out interviewing kinks ahead of time.

_____   _____   10. Having a life goal is little help when it comes to finding and winning the right job.

TOTAL CORRECT ☐

ANSWERS: (1) True (2) False (3) True (4) True (5) True (6) True (7) False (8) True (9) True (10) False

Score 10 points for correct answers. You have excellent knowledge and retention if you earned 80% or above. A score of less than 60% suggests you should review materials relating to missed questions again.

PLAN B:

Protecting Your Career From The Winds of Change

> *"Life is a series of collisions with the future; it is not a sum of what we have been but what we yearn to be."*
>
> *Jose' Ortega y Gasset*

VIEW YOUR CAREER
FROM A NEW PERSPECTIVE

Please erase from your memory bank any preconceived ideas you may have regarding career growth and job changes and open your mind to a new, innovative approach that will help you view work from a more exciting perspective. A growth program (Plan B) as conceived and introduced on these pages is far more than an alternate or contingency job plan should your present one fall apart. Rather, it is a broad-based, intelligent personal growth program that can take you (1) to a more significant role in your present organization, or (2) lead you to a better position elsewhere, and (3) assist you in making giant strides in the direction of your life goal. And all of this can take place while you remain in your present job. The risk is minimal.

The material ahead should be read with a pencil in hand because, within one hour, you will have started your Plan B and, henceforth, will view work and your career in a more positive, exciting way.

PART 1

WHAT IS A PLAN B?

Plan B is nothing more than a career insurance policy. Properly developed, it will provide a cushion against the shocks of future changes, such as unexpected unemployment. A plan B as described in this book, is a carefully researched and designed strategy to provide an immediate and exciting opportunity should your present job (Plan A) lose its luster or disappear. A Plan B is not a temporary alternative or substitute job should problems arise. It is a reserve program that can match or be superior to your Plan A (present job). And it is more!

View Plan B as having a large sum of money salted away in an investment of your choice. You may never draw on the account, but it is there if you become unhappy with your present situation. And, just as well invested money draws interest or pays dividends while held in reserve, so does a Plan B. For example, the very existance of a Plan B growth program can cause you to feel more independent (and secure) about your present job. This in turn, can cause you to be more confident and thereby do better at it. It can also give your present job (whatever it may be) more meaning and help you make progress toward a life goal. These, and other significant benefits to be explored in the pages ahead, are not normally seen or understood. But they exist and can guarantee that you receive a high rate of interest from your investment. In other words, a Plan B growth program will add new assets to your "career bank."

Despite these and other advantages, most people wait on the sidelines without developing a diversified career "contingency plan." In doing this, they put all of their career eggs into one basket. This is foolish when you consider that a Plan B can help a Plan A prosper.

THE ANATOMY OF A PLAN B

A Plan B is a comprehensive, detailed, and realistic career plan that can be activated within a few days. It is a seven step strategy that has been planned in advance so if your present job (Plan A) disappears, or you wish to leave it behind, you have replacement choices. These will be in harmony with your abilities, talents, interests, and life goals.

A Plan B growth program is more than an idea in the back of your mind. It must be fully researched and planned in writing. Key contacts must also be developed as your Plan B is formulated. Although it may sound like doing a homework assignment, it is far more exciting and the benefits are greater and more immediate. Ideally, your Plan B can be developed while you are improving your Plan A. Many successful people devote several hours each week over a period of months to develop and refine a high quality Plan B.

And they enjoy the challenge!

THE WINDS OF CHANGE

For many people a Plan B would have been a good idea twenty years ago. But, then few people were thinking in that direction. Ten years ago such a plan would have been an excellent strategy. Those who developed one outdistanced others. Today Plan B is virtually mandatory. Read the daily paper and you soon realize there is no immunity from changes that can render either your job or your organization obsolete.

What our parents used to call a "secure job" is extinct. Changes have been so dramatic in recent years that even if you own and operate a small business, economic, social, political or legal changes can suddenly throw you into bankruptcy. Perhaps trends change, or maybe rent or insurance rates explode. Life simply doesn't come with guarantees.

Alvin Toffler in his book *Future Shock* (published in 1971) predicted changes that seemed revolutionary. Many of the changes he predicted arrived so fast that Mr. Toffler published a second book soon thereafter titled *The Third Wave* to catch up on the wild winds of change. Toffler did an outstanding job describing the large changes to the country. Most people were unable, however, to consider how those changes would affect their lives. Only a few individuals took Toffler's predictions personally.

In addition to external changes (such as those described by Toffler) there are changes within individuals. Sometimes a person reaches a "crisis point" where a new life goal appears and career adjustments need to be made. At other times, job dissatisfaction becomes accute and a change becomes a necessity.

Are the winds of change blowing in your life today? What impact will they have on your future? On the following pages are some causes (winds) that may sweep you off your feet.

Are you ready for them?

WINDS THAT COULD BLOW YOUR JOB AWAY

RESTRUCTURING: Almost all major organizations are streamlining to lower overhead and become more competitive. World competition for established markets are responsible. Some organizations started this process earlier than others. They were wise. The result for these organizations was more gradual change and fewer layoffs. Today, no organization is immune. Everyone has had to adjust. Some firms have helped retrain employees for new jobs; others have simply cut their workforce. This "downsizing" has had a sobering effect upon employee morale. Some of the more fortunate employees received special severance incentives (known as "golden handshakes") or were provided with professional "outplacement counseling" to help them adjust. Others were simply handed a "pink slip" and left to fend for themselves. Very few of those laid-off had a workable Plan B in the wings.

MERGERS: in a merger two organizations decide to join forces to become more efficient or enter new markets. Often one company is in financial trouble and is taken over by a healthy corporation. The term often used during a merger is consolidation. Savings occur when two offices are combined into one. But people pay the price because two sets of employees, (such as office staff) are not usually needed. Someone has to go or change jobs and seniority or talent do not always count.

CHANGES-CHANGES-CHANGES

DISLOCATIONS: Economic pressures sometimes make it necessary for an organization to relocate its offices or plants. Sometimes organizations move from New York because of high salaries and rent to less expensive places such as Texas, or Kentucky. It makes good sense economically, but in the process many people are left behind. Often many can't (or won't) move. They resist the winds of change. If they do not have a Plan B in reserve, they must scramble.

POLITICAL: Everyone is familiar with political change. Smart people always have a Plan B in Washington, D.C., Partisan employees face the strongest political winds. Civil Service provides job security, but even here changes are being considered. Political winds accelerate economic and social changes that can affect everyone.

SOCIAL: Double income families are more vulnerable to change than when there is a single wage earner. If the primary breadwinner loses his or her job, it often means this person has to find suitable employment elsewhere. Result? Two people need a Plan B rather than one. Social winds have indirectly created a greater need for alternative career plans.

COMPETITION FROM IMMIGRANTS: The American economy is not only adjusting to foreign competition on products, it also faces competition from immigrants. We have a growing number of people from other nations joining our workforce. Many are willing to work harder than the typical American worker and consequently they absorb entry level jobs which can be a springboard to more responsible positions later.

All of the winds of change mentioned add up to a compelling need for smart workers to have a well-designed Plan B. It is no longer *if* you get caught up on the whirlwind of change that might result in a change in your job status, it is being prepared for *when*.

JULIE

Julie was so tired of rumors about cutbacks that there was a certain amount of relief when her firm finally declared bankruptcy and eliminated her position. She immediately signed up for unemployment insurance payments and took a two-week "vacation". Then she started a job hunting expedition.

Things didn't go well. For one thing, Julie wasn't prepared mentally for a job search. Even worse, she had allowed some of her basic skills to deteriorate. As a result, Julie became discouraged and lost her confidence. It took her over a year (including several college classes) to get her once promising career back on track.

Julie made the classic mistake of thinking she could use unemployment insurance as a security blanket. She felt a new job would be easy to find. What she failed to understand is that developing a Plan A from scratch is far more difficult than developing a Plan B while you are still working. If Julie had worked on a fleasible growth program before her position was eliminated, she could have enjoyed her vacation and returned prepared to locate a better position than she left. With a solid Plan B her one year "down period" would have been eliminated.

If you dislike trying to find a job on a full-time basis, a growth program prepared ahead of time is your best possible strategy.

PLAN B BEGINS
WITH A PHILOSOPHY

It would be a mistake to consider a career growth program (prepared while in your present job) simply as a blueprint to take you through a difficult transition period into another job or career. It is equally important to view such a plan as an attitude. The mind set for Plan B says one must not depend exclusively on others (especially managers in large organizations) to develop and protect your future. A good Plan B is a ''take care of yourself'' project. It is an attitude that acknowledges change is inevitable and no job or career is 100% secure. It is an attitude that recognizes the danger in becoming too comfortable with any career role and the acceptance that alternatives are necessary to avoid becoming vulnerable to the winds of change.

Obviously, change can be a barrier from reaching a life goal. Change can send a person on a detour from which a return to the main highway is difficult. Thus a Plan B philosophy says: ''No matter how strong the winds may be, you cannot allow them to blow away your future. You must ride out the storm, adjust, and be true to your future.''

Plan B is basically a way to interpret the modern world which will give you a better chance to reach your life goals. The ''good old days'' of company loyalty, and promotion from within, are not as realistic as they once were. The rules have changed. The game is played differently. And without a Plan B you risk leaving yourself open to frustration and despair.

The good news about constructing a career growth program is that the philosophy you develop will enhance other aspects of your life. Some examples of this are provided on the next page.

THE PLAN B HABIT

Some years ago my wife and I were traveling in Europe when student riots in France prevented us from following our scheduled plan. Stranded in London, and feeling sorry for ourselves, we came up with an alternate plan to visit Scotland. We had a glorious time and that experience caused us to form the ''Plan B'' habit.

Although the material in this book deals with the benefits of developing a career Plan B (and how to do it), you will also see the advantages in other situations. For example, a Plan B is desirable:

- When a financial reverse occurs.
- When another individual lets you down.
- When unexpected company arrives.
- When a college major turns sour.
- When your dentist retires.
- When your favorite restaurant is closed.
- When a computer fails.
- When your car breaks down.
- When your flight is cancelled.

Almost every plan you make could use a Plan B to provide flexibility and prevent frustration. In developing a Plan B for career and life goal purposes, you will see the advantages (and improve your skills) in having a backup strategy in every day situations. Result? The unexpected ''bumps'' of living will be easier to handle.

> **THOSE WITH A PLAN B IN PLACE USUALLY WIND UP HAPPIER IN THE WORKPLACE AND LESS SUSCEPTIBLE TO JOB BURNOUT**

THE CHALLENGE!

The foundation of the Plan B philosophy is the development of a learning attitude that says: ''I will start learning more about my specific career area and the opportunities it provides from a variety of sources. These sources include key people I know or will meet in the future. It means learning more about my present job including seminars and self-learning. I accept that only by keeping my skills current can I avoid a major ''catch up'' period in the future—a period that could measurably slow my career progress.

PART 2

THE SEVEN STEP STRATEGY

ANTICIPATING THE WINDS OF CHANGE

This section contains seven steps that will lead you through a successful Plan B growth program. Although all seven steps are recommended, you may decide to eliminate one or two or place more emphasis on some. Every situation is different. Each individual has his or her own form of interpretation and style. After all, the future you are dealing with is your own!

YOU'LL NEVER COMPLETE A PLAN B IF YOU VIEW IT AS WORK—YOU'VE GOT ENOUGH OF THAT ALREADY. TIE IT TO YOUR LIFE GOAL AND MAKE IT A CHALLENGE. IT CAN EVEN BE FUN!

THE SEVEN STEP STRATEGY

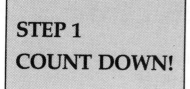

STEP 1

COUNT DOWN!

(How to design a support system to help you complete a Plan B.)

Few individuals who promise themselves to complete a growth plan actually do so because they lack a support system. Without such a system it is easy for a Plan B to become "just talk".

> Genevieve had slowly turned off her friends and co-workers through constant talk about getting a teaching credential, but never doing anything about it. Her best friend, Rachel, finally decided to address the situation and said: "Look, Gen, we are all tired of talk without any action. Why don't you do something about your future or forget it? I'll make you a wager. When you get your credential I'll buy you dinner at the best restaurant in town. Between now and then, promise you won't keep talking about how you're going to get your credential. Deal?"

Like Genevieve, most people need all the motivation they can muster to start and complete a Plan B. What kind of motivation would you require? And equally important, what kind of support from others would be necessary to convert what is in your mind to action? On the next page are four options. If you feel that one is the kind of support you would favorably respond to, place a check in the appropriate square. If none appeal to you, design your own plan in the spaces provided.*

---

*Should the reader feel that a support system of any kind is unnecesary, he or she is reminded that a Plan B must be developed while a Plan A is kept in full operation and one's lifestyle is maintained. It is something you do on top of everything else. It is not business as usual and that is why an advance support strategy (especially if there is some excitement to it) may be best for some people.

DESIGN A SUPPORT SYSTEM

☐ **Option #1: USE THE POWER OF SECRECY.** For some individuals, getting others to provide support would demonstrate weakness on their part and do more harm that good. These people like to prove to others, (especially superiors), that they are independently strong and disciplined. Thus the more secrecy surrounding the project the more motivated these individuals become. It is the fact that they do not discuss their Plan B with others until they can make a big announcement at the end (after completion) that provides the motivating goal.

☐ **Option #2: COMMIT YOURSELF TO OTHERS.** This option is in juxtoposition to number one. Some individuals find the movitation they require is obtained by openly communicating their plan to those most important in their lives. Not having to ''back down'' from a commitment (and winding up with the ''guilts'') is what causes these people to complete a project. They purposely create their own trap and then make certain they are not caught in it!

☐ **Option #3: ARRANGE A PERSONAL CONTRACT.** This works when there is a significant person who is willing to provide support and counseling on a regular basis. Spouses, close friends, or mentors work well. The idea is to make a verbal (or written) agreement to meet at regular intervals to evaluate progress until the Plan B is complete. For many individuals, this options works well.

☐ **Option #4: CHOOSE A SMALL, SELECT SUPPORT GROUP.** Those who prefer this approach like to share their Plan B with a select group of individuals who can be called upon for guidance and support. It is like doing a long-distance swim and having people at both ends and along your side to cheer you on as you make the effort. Structure in the form of regular progress reports can be added if desired. Here again, care in the selection of support people is critical. Only those who will take the assignment seriously should be given consideration.

☐ **Option #5: DOING IT WITH OTHERS.** For some a partnership or team arrangement is the best of all. Besides the fun that can occur sharing and working together, mutual support is nice to have. The primary problem with a "partnership approach" is that one party may be more serious and professional than the other to produce a viable Plan B. A team or partnership effort may work, but it may be wise to reserve one of the other options in case is doesn't.

☐ **Option #6: SELF-DESIGNED STRATEGY.** Please write out the option you prefer. If desired, use a combination of those suggested above.

_____

_____

_____

_____

_____

_____

Once you have your support system in place you are ready to prepare a Plan B for launching at a later date. The more you anticipate this event the more motivated you will be to get there!

CASE #11	RICHARD

When Richard came home from Viet Nam it was his Uncle George who introduced him to the President of Barr Manufacturing who offered Richard a job. Since then Richard has made slow but steady progress with Barr. He is now Traffic Manager (and loves it) but is worried for two reasons. (1) He needs to measurably upgrade his statistical skills to keep the job. (2) Rumor has it that Barr may sell out to a larger company.

Richard has been thinking about developing a Plan B for two years but lacks enough motivation to get started. Last night, in a discussion with his wife Marie, it was decided he should adopt one of these strategies.

(1) Ask Uncle George if he will sign an informal contract that commits Richard to report on his progress every two weeks. Richard has so much respect for his Uncle that it would be most difficult to let him down. Besides, Uncle George is knowledgable and could provide expert guidance until his Plan B is finished.

(2) Create a small support group by asking the following individuals if they would be available to talk with him should his progress "bog down".

> —Marie
> —His superior at work with whom he has a
>   "mentor" type relationship.
> —Jack, his best friend.
> —Neighbor Fred who is a retired teacher.
> —Uncle George

Which strategy would you support?

_____

_____

_____

_____

See page 213 for author's comments.

STEP 2
HEDGE YOUR CAREER BET

(Free yourself to do a Plan B by streamlining your Plan A)

Frequently an individual will fix up a home or autombile to sell, then, after the improvements have been made, change his or her mind. The home or car turns out to be better than what is available for the same price in the marketplace. Why not keep it?

The same thing can happen in preparing a growth plan. When you have finished with it, your Plan A (present job) looks so much better than when you started you decide to keep it. This is most apt to occur when you streamline your Plan A to work on Plan B.

> When Jill first heard a friend say the best way to get ready to leave a job is to become better at it, she almost flipped. Yet, after discussing the idea at length Jill agreed. The premise is basic. By becoming more effective at Plan A it ceases to be a drag on the preparation of a Plan B. Then, if Plan B does not work out, you can fall back on an improved Plan A and still come out ahead. Some people call this hedging. Jill decided to follow this strategy.

It stands to reason that developing a workable Plan B will take time, energy, and mental effort. But does it need to be a burden? The answer is no, providing you relieve some of the pressure by becoming more effective in your present job. In other words, streamline what you do so you become more efficient and it takes less out of you.

As contradictory as it may at first seem, your second step is to improve the way you are dealing with your Plan A. To assist you in doing this twenty possible efficiency measures are listed on the next page. It is recognized that work situations are vastly different, so some of the suggestions may not apply.

STREAMLINING YOUR PLAN A

Place a check in a few of the boxes listed below and you will be gaining time to work more seriously on your Plan B.

☐ Curtail excessive socialization on the job. Stay friendly but back away a little.

☐ Concentrate on your job and let others worry about problems beyond your control.

☐ Become more professional as a worker. Look and act the part.

☐ Become a more positive person. Let negative views and rumors bounce off you.

☐ Work hard to increase personal productivity. A drop in your productivity can be counter-productive in building a Plan B.

☐ Work to restore any negative relationships that exist. These cause an energy drain which could be put to better use elsewhere.

☐ Eliminate obvious time-wasters that have become habits (such as an afternoon coffee break).

☐ Insulate yourself against unsolvable human problems that are draining you.

☐ Do a better job of balancing home and career responsibilities.

☐ If you are a manager, start delegating more. If you are not a manager spend less time carrying the work load of others.

☐ Take a stronger stand with superiors on accepting new responsibilities. Refuse to let others unload on you. Carry your full share of work but take a firm stand against overloads.

- [ ] Use your lunch break (or other down time) to work on Plan B.

- [ ] Start building stronger relationships with those who may be in a position to help you launch your Plan B later.

- [ ] Start an exercise program.

- [ ] Improve your absentee record.

- [ ] Establish (in writing) daily work priorities.

- [ ] Whatever it takes to build a better relationship with your supervisor, do it. The less strain that falls on you from above the easier the building of your Plan B will be.

- [ ] Shorten business telephone conversations. Cut back on personal calls.

- [ ] Dress for success. Looking more efficient may help you become more efficient.

Your goal is to develop a Plan B that will improve your career, get you a better job, and take you closer to your life goal. With less stress coming from your Plan A you will be free to do this and improve your future.

If it sounds like too much work, talk it over with a support person. Perhaps there is some way you can convert the streamlining you have in mind to a challenge with a reward at the end.

CASE #12	CONFLICT

Although James and Gregg are good friends they occasionally get into some highly emotional arguments over career strategies. Yesterday, over lunch, they had a beauty when Gregg said.

"James, you might as well quit now, take a vacation, and come back looking for a new job. You miss the whole idea of using your present job as a platform to gain a better one. You can't seem to get it through your brain that becoming better at what you are doing here will improve your attitude toward outside opportunities. Right now you are cutting off your nose to spite your face."

"Look big shot", replied James, "you don't know how negative I have become about this job. I feel I am in a pressure cooker and management is turning the gas higher. Then, you sit there and tell me to take a fresh look at what I am dong to benefit myself. My guess is that 95% of people who turn sour on a job quit without having a decent plan. That's the way the system works. The only way I am going to benefit myself is to quit and take that vacation you are talking about. I will never prepare for another job until the pressure is totally off me here. As far as I am concerned, you can take your Plan B and stuff it in your ear."

Would you defend James or Gregg? Write your answer in the space below and then compare your answers to that of the author on page 213.

_____

_____

_____

STEP 3
YOU'VE GOT TO BE KIDDING!

(Your present job can provide more than money or benefits while you work on your Plan B)

This step encourages you to view your current job as a place where you can continue to learn. This holds true even if you feel boxed in, or mad at your boss, or even if you don't expect to hang around for long.

Some employees become so discouraged about their current jobs that they do not recognize some of the on-site learning opportunities that are present. A few, once they become serious about a Plan B, take a second look and discover a wide variety of learning opportunities exist. When this happens, they often reverse their previous attitude and start improving old skills while learning new ones. Of course, this doesn't happen to everyone. Rather than viewing their Plan A as a paid learning station for the duration (the smart approach) some people continue to see it as a bummer-job leading nowhere. These individuals needlessly victimize themselves.

Streamlining your Plan A (Step 2) may have already contributed to a more positive attitude toward your current job and this may have uncovered some learning opportunities you have failed to see in the past. If so, step in and learn all you can. Continue to search for new assignments and new relationships with people who have something important to teach you. The more you learn, the better things will turn out for you in the future. Easy to say, hard to do!

PSYCHOLOGICAL BLOCKS

One reason you may not have taken advantage of learning opportunities in the past is because you may have some psychological "blocks" to overcome. For example, blocks frequently occur among mature employees in a high tech field (like computer science). These individuals are fully capable of learning new technology but have permitted the never ending advancement of technology to form barriers in their mind and they give up.

There are three steps to overcoming learning blocks: (1) Recognize you may have one. (2) Make up your mind to reverse the problem. (3) Find help to master what needs to be learned.

There is another kind of mental block. When a change occurs in the work environment some employees always seem to consider it bad no matter what the change may be. As a result, they develop a negative attitude (mental block) against it. Other colleagues have learned to view change as an opportunity not a problem. This attitude allows them to open their minds, learn new methods or skills and prepare for better jobs ahead. These individuals are not just "putting in time", they are preparing themselves for the future.

What can you learn from your present job? It depends upon where you are, the freedom you have, and what new learning opportunities surround you. Sometimes, after careful analysis, you may discover your job environment may not provide any new learning opportunities despite your best effort. If this turns out to be the case, you should move on to step 5.

LEARNING SOURCES

To help you identify learning sources from your present job, please complete the following exercise. Place a ☑ opposite any learning opportunity that can be developed.

☐ Ask your supervisor for some new responsibilities where new learning possibilities exist. One idea is to start with a task co-workers do not want.

☐ Go on record requesting to learn how to operate a piece of equipment or software, where you have little or no experience. Sometimes it is possible to learn this on your own time.

☐ Investigate the opportunities of company sponsored seminars or training that you can attend or take.

☐ Ask a colleague who is a specialist to help you develop some new skills.

☐ Identify accessible individuals whom you can learn from through informal meetings, interviews, and coffee breaks. Some people are better resources than books.

Each work environment has its own learning opportunities. All it takes is a motivated person who is willing to discover and absorb knowledge. This usually means asking the right questions at the right time from the right people. Although formal education and self-learning outside of work will also contribute to your future, there is nothing that can replace the on-the-job training and experience most organizations provide.

> **It's nice to earn
> while you learn.**

CASE #13	ATTITUDE REVERSAL

When Tanya started with her firm two years ago she made some serious mistakes. First, she learned only what was necessary for her to get the basic job done. Nothing extra. Second, she made some unnecessary human relation errors. As a result, she is currently at odds with her supervisor and has a serious conflict with two co-workers. Because she got herself off to such a bad start, Tanya has decided to develop a Plan B.

Tanya's first move was to start taking advantage of learning opportunities she neglected in the past. This included qualifying to operate three pieces of office equipment with which she was unfamiliar. She also recognized a need for greater concentration on her English skills to reduce her level of mistakes. Finally, Tanya decided to work hard to improve her relationship with her supervisor and co-workers. Tanya admits that doing all of this will mean a major behavioral change on her part, but she views it as an integral part of developing a Plan B. Besides, it is never too late to change.

What success do you predict for Tanya?

☐ Tanya will become discouraged and leave her job before her Plan B is complete.

☐ Tanya will succeed and after her Plan B is complete she will move on to a much better job.

To compare your views to that of the author, please turn to page 213.

STEP 4
QUALIFY FIRST!

(Then and only then are you officially in the race.)

In most athletic contests (cycling races, 10K's, swimming events etc.) one must qualify to compete for the recognition and prizes offered. The same is true in the career race. To qualify, a person must verify and reach current job skill standards. Those who do not do this may *think* they are in the race, but the truth is they have disqualified themselves before starting.

Every job specialty has its own compentency standards. A compentency is nothing more than a skill that can be observed and measured. There are technical skills *and* human relations skills. Although human-relations skills are not as easy to quantify as technical skills, they are equally important.

The problem with job compentencies in a dynamic society is that they are constantly upgraded by the job market. Professionals understand this and strive to keep their skills up to standard or above. Non-professionals allow their compentencies to slip.

Both Hazel and Florence use applications software in their positions as financial analysts. Hazel has a great attitude toward learning. Through self-instruction and formal classes she keeps current with the newest software. Florence, has a get-by learning attitude. She depends greatly on the help of others to keep her job.

If both of their jobs should be eliminated, Hazel would be "market ready" for another job. Florence would not.

WHERE ARE YOU?

Where are you? Do you need to do a market skills analysis to see if you have
fallen behind in your specialty? If so, this effort should be a part of your Plan B
program. To assist you in doing this, the following three part strategy is
recommended.

| FIRST | Write out what you believe to be the present compentencies required
to keep you competitive in your job speciality. Include both technical
and human skills.

_____

_____

_____

_____

_____

_____

_____

_____

_____

VERIFY

NEXT Verify your list by consulting with placement or human resource professionals (your local college counselor can help direct you to such a person). This, in effect, will constitute a skill analysis. Add new compentencies you need to learn. Delete those no longer required.

THEN Make a list of any compentencies where upgrading is required to make you competitive.

_____

_____

_____

_____

_____

_____

_____

_____

_____

CASE #14	JACK'S PROBLEM

When Jack finally got around to verifying the skills he would need to compete effectively for a job that was consistant with his life goal, he realized just how far behind he was. He knew some upgrading was due when he started, but when he took a close look at his list, Jack was tempted to give up.

Then it occured to him that he had two options. His first option would be to divide the competencies he needed into three groups. In Group 1 Jack would include those skills he could learn from his present job; Group 2 would include those competencies he could learn from self-study efforts at home; Group 3 would include those that he could learn only from more formal training, probably from evening courses at the local college.

His second option would be to quit his present job and return to campus full time. In this manner he could "catch up" more quickly and then start over with a new job. This option would put a strain on Jack's finances and curtail his lifestyle but would not be impossible.

What other factors should Jack consider in making his decision? Which option would you recommend? Why?

Compare your thinking with the author's on page 213.

STEP 5
DECISION TIME

(What will it be? Back to campus, self-instruction or both?)

When it comes to reaching new competency goals in order to maintain market mobility, most people have a choice. They can either go on campus (enroll in a night program) or undertake a self-instructional program at home. Once you have given careful consideration to the factors below you are invited to make the decision that is best for you.

FORMAL TRAINING AS A BRIDGE TO PLAN B

Most people find it necessary or advisable to obtain academic preparation to reach their Plan B. Sometimes (as in obtaining a license to practice medicine) this preparation can take years. Some professions require a degree to qualify for entry. At other times, a single course can do the trick.

Consider the following cases.

Jason's Plan B is to become a second level manager for a State agency. So far Jason has taken advantage of every in-service training program available. He also asks for additional responsibilities when there is some ''new learning'' involved. But Jason faces a serious problem in the future because he cannot speak Spanish. Co-workers and clients are increasingly Hispanic. Two weeks ago Jason enrolled in Spanish I at a local community college. He knows reaching his Plan B depends upon his becoming bilingual.

Six years ago Joan was a secretary in an architectural firm. Today she is an architect in the same organization. Developing a Plan B is responsible for the transition. Joan realized her career at that firm was at a dead-end. Six years ago, she started fooling with a Plan B and, as a result, took a course called Architecture I at a local state college. The instructor was so enthusiastic and understanding that Joan became hooked. With the full cooperation of her firm, she completed the total curriculum. Academic training was her bridge between being a secretary and an architect.

Beth (a saleswoman in a department store) and her husband Ken (a bank manager) designed a program to establish a small business of their own. Their academic preparation consisted of taking a college course at night called Successful Small Business Operation. The course project consisted of setting up a hypothetical business on paper. The professor allowed Beth and Ken to work as a team. When the course was over Beth quit her job first to get things started while Ken's salary continued. Ken joined Beth after two years. Although the academic training was minimal, without it Beth and Ken would not have received the necessary foundation to establish a successful business.

RETURN TO CAMPUS?

Does your Plan B involve additional formal education? If so, it should be encouraging for you to know the many advantages (some you may not be aware of) of returning to any campus that can provide what you need. These advantages apply whether or not you already have a degree. Please ☑ any of the benefits listed below which you were not aware of when you started the exercise.

☐ In some *career fields* college is the best place to increase compentency.

☐ Many adults who return to college do so with great anxiety, however, it is hard to find anyone later who regretted the decision.

☐ A college campus is an ideal place to network.

☐ Every person can improve his or her ability to communicate. A college campus is a great place to accomplish this goal.

☐ College professors often make excellent mentors.

☐ Colleges provide a wide variety of support services (including those taking a single course). These services include learning centers where individual tutoring is available, career guidance centers, job-placement counseling, etc. A college campus is often the best source for such services.

☐ Colleges offer many short non-credit courses so individuals can upgrade themselves at a modest cost.

☐ Graduation from high school is not always a requirement for entrance to a college program.

☐ Colleges often help their students improve self-esteem.

DO-IT-YOURSELF LEARNING

Self-study is a growing way to reach competency goals contained in a Plan B. Michelle is a case in point.

Michelle has just about exhausted the learning opportunities in her present job. Because she is a single parent raising two children, she cannot easily attend courses at the local university. She has not, however, lost her enthusiasm for her Plan B. Two or three nights each week, after the children are in bed. Michelle devotes a minimum of one hour to her own self-development. She selects publications that will lead in the direction of her Plan B. Currently she is taking a correspondence course in Beginning Supervision. Michelle's goal is to become an Administrative Officer in the small school district where she is employed.

In discussing her self-development program with her boss, Michelle made this statement: "Reading and studying self-help books fits into my lifestyle. After the day is over and there is some quiet time, I can sit down with a cup of coffee and make excellent progress. Sometimes I can apply what I have learned the following day. My future plans do not call for an academic degree but, if needed in the future, I can list the self-help subjects covered in my resume just as if I had attended a class. Some people who find it impossible to attend formal college classes give up on future progress. This is foolish. Self-learning has many advantages. You pick your own subjects and set your own pace. Of course, it takes self-discipline but what kind of education doesn't?"

All you need do is visit your local public library or a commercial book store and browse through the various self-help books that are available for your consideration. As an example, the publisher of this book specializes in self-study books. A list of those books can be found at the back of this book.

IT IS POSSIBLE TO DO BOTH!

Of course, some individuals (in addition to what they learn on the job), return to campus for courses and engage in self-instructional programs at the same time. These people wisely design their own curriculum to meet their specific goals. As a guide to your own educational program please complete the following:

I plan to return to campus to complete these courses:

_____

_____

_____

I plan to use self-help publications to upgrade myself in these areas:

_____

_____

_____

Lifelong learning has become a reality. To those in retirement, learning for the sake of learning is an enviable attitude; for those who remain in the workplace new learning is often a necessity. The winds of change dictate the curriculum.

IT IS A MISTAKE TO ASSUME YOUR PRESENT COMPETENCIES WILL TAKE YOU ALL THE WAY TO RETIREMENT

CASE #15	A CHALLENGE FOR MARY

Mary accepted a position as a clerk/receptionist with a major supermarket organization because it was the only job immediately available as her husband started a new legal practice. Mary figures the Liberal Arts degree she had would stand her in good stead even though her clerical skills were underdeveloped.

Mary soon became intrigued with the Marketing Department and decided her creative talents could be put to good use in that area. As a receptionist she knew Ralph Dillon, Vice President in charge of marketing. One morning as Mr. Dillon entered the building she asked if she could speak with him. He gave her a time to meet. The meeting determined the following skills that Mary would need to achieve before she would be a candidate to join the marketing department.

> High level knowledge of applications software.
> More graphics experience in layout and design.
> A course in market research.
> Better understanding of coupon marketing.
> A course on consumer behavior.

Overwhelmed by the list, Mary decided to think twice about the idea. A few days later, Mr. Dillion saw Mary and said, "You would already have some of the skills we discussed had you been a marketing major, but frankly, I like the creativity of your liberal arts background. All of the skills we listed can be learned at night at our local university or through some self-help materials I can provide. Are you still interested?"

Does this constitute a good Plan B for Mary? What suggestions would you make as far as implementation? Please write out your answers and compare with those on page 214.

STEP 6
CREATIVE NETWORKING

To win a better job it is recommended that you seek the professional assistance of a qualified placement agency. Their contacts may help you, especially if you have an application and resume.

Although placement agencies have helped thousands of people, never forget that the best strategy is to depend upon yourself. Translated, this means you should think of yourself as your own employment agency. There are employers who are seeking people with certain skills. Just like an employment agency, you will gain your best results by marketing yourself through creative networking.

You have a major advantage over others because you have completed a Plan B. Although you may not have thought about it, your plan can constitute the secret formula you need. The following four strategies will help you establish your own "employment agency."

FOR THOSE NEW TO NETWORKING

Networking involves building relationships with knowledgable professionals in your career area of interest who are in a position to lead you to a new and better job opportunity. You may include placement directors on your networking list but most should be people in the field to which you aspire. Some may be in your present company. Others may work for competitors.

Relationships you build should be mutually rewarding. This means you must look for ways to repay them (if only in gratitude) so they are willing to go out of their way to assist you.

Building such a network should start as early as possible, because you may need these key individuals to help you market your plan once it is complete. How do you go about networking? Here are some suggestions. Place a ☑ opposite those you can be enthusiastic about.

☐ Joining a trade or professional association in your career area. Attend meetings. Make new friends. Learn what is going on. Where the career opportunities are.

☐ Attend conferences where you can meet other professionals in your area. Find out about any Plan B's they have.

☐ Attend formal classes, seminars, or workshops and make new friends so you can exchange career information with them.

☐ Make the effort to create a mentor or two within your present organization.

☐ Start spending time with some Plan B enthusiasts in your or other organizations.

☐ Contact professionals and arrange informational interviews to gain their suggestions on how to activate your Plan B when it is ready.

STRATEGIES AHEAD →

STRATEGY 1
BECOME A CAREER
INFORMATION MAGNET

First you need to understand what is going on in the marketplace of your career specialty. What changes are taking place? What needs are not being filled? What new areas of expertise are employers seeking? What salary and benefit packages are being offered?

There are many ways to accumulate this kind of data. Check those below that have appeal.

☐ Become more active in trade associations. Attend meetings with "networking" in mind.

☐ Join other, related trade associations.

☐ Have lunch or after-work social meetings with knowledgeable people who are also information magnets.

☐ Subscribe to and study appropriate trade magazines.

☐ Attend trade conferences.

☐ Create a resource contact on your local campus.

☐ Share what you learn with others so they, in turn, will share with you.

☐ Do nice things for your "network sources" and enjoy doing it.

☐ Other: _____

_____

_____

The whole idea is to play the information game so that you are not left on the sidelines uninformed.

STRATEGY 2
REFINE AND EXPAND NETWORKING
WITH INFORMATION INTERVIEWS

The more key people you can locate who are willing to discuss your career plans with you, or recommend you to others, the better. With a list of such people "working for you" you start to cover the market and your self-employment program moves into high gear. Not only does networking mean your calling on others, when you create good allies, they may call you. When your Plan B is nearing completion it is time to use networking to put the finishing touches to it. Those in your "camp" can help you refine it now and maintain it in the future. This can best be accomplished through information interviews.

An information interview is designed primarily to "test the market" on various issues such as competency standards, employment conditions, what employers are really seeking, etc. Although an information interview can be the first step finding a new opportunity, it is extremely valuable in its own right. Information interviews usually add fresh names to your networking system. They are also other advantages. Naturally, any information interview that leads to an *employment interview* falls into this category.

The key to gaining an information interview is your own attitude. If you are sincere in seeking information and communicate you will be most appreciative should you receive it, chances are good the interview will be yours. Keep in mind that it is difficult for a person who has achieved status in a career field to turn a newcomer down when they ask for advice you are in a unique position to provide. Here are some tips.

☐ Seek people who are in key roles but not directly associated with employment. They receive fewer opportunities to help newcomers.

☐ Approach the interview with an open mind so you can discover new possibilities each time.

☐ Arrange to meet with them on their conditions (if appropriate offer to host them for lunch).

☐ Mention that you have a Plan B and would like advice regarding it.

☐ Listen carefully to all suggestions. Ask relevant questions.

☐ Ask who else might be in a position to provide you with insights and advice.

☐ Always send a "thank you" message.

☐ If appropriate, convert the beginning relationship into a mutually rewarding long-term one.

☐ Do not "press" beyond the individuals willingness to volunteer information and advice.

STRATEGY 3
EMPLOY AN "ENDLESS CHAIN" NETWORK SYSTEM

Regardless of the kind of networking you have done in the past, consider using an endless chain system. Below is a diagram. Start by listing three key people you feel would be receptive to looking at your Plan B, who are in a position to know of job openings in your specialty. Call each name and make a best effort to arrange a personal meeting. Mention you are completing your Plan B (this may intrigue them) and if you are successful, take it with you.

Once in conversation, request additional names so that you can start your chain. Names provided should be people with whom the first party has an excellent relationship. Always ask if you can use the individual's name. With effort on your part, the "endless chain" networking system can live up to its name. You can keep it operational even after your Plan B turns into Plan A.

"ENDLESS CHAIN" NETWORKING

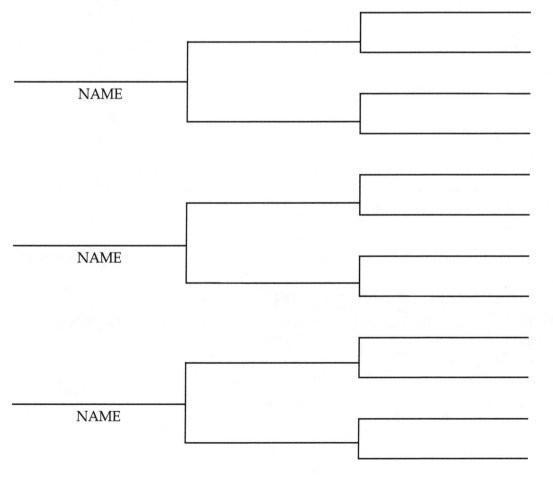

NAME

NAME

NAME

| CASE #16 | THE CONTACT THAT PAID OFF |

Donna had been working undercover on her Plan B for over six months when her boss Mrs. MacCarthy came down hard on her over a mistake a co-worker made. At that moment Donna decided to activate her Plan B.

The first person she decided to call was a Ms. Jamison, a Human Resource director for an electronics firm near her home. Donna met Ms. Jamison through a mutual friend, Hazel, at a conference on job burnout a few weeks earlier. Donna had to make four calls to reach Ms. Jamison (her secretary kept saying she was in a conference) but when the contact was made, Ms. Jamison was most receptive to an information interview and made an appointment for the following week.

The moment Ms. Jamison knew that Donna had almost completed her Plan B she showed immediate interest and they wound up having lunch together. Although Ms. Jamison's firm did not have an opening suitable for Donna, she knew of another firm who did and made arrangements for Donna to be interviewed by a Mr. Sledge.

Donna's qualifications (having been upgraded through her Plan B) were ideal and an employment offer was made which Donna accepted with enthusiasm.

Donna's friend Hazel seemed bored and negative when she heard the story during lunch the following week. Hazel's comments: ''You really lucked out, Donna. What happened to you seldom, if ever, happens to others. Frankly, I think networking of all kinds is overrated.''

Do you agree with Hazel? Compare your thoughts with those of the author on page 214.

STEP 7
HAVE PLAN—WILL TRAVEL

This final step provides techniques on how to use your Plan B to win a better position either at your present firm or with another organization.

At this stage everything you know or have experienced about job hunting and employment interviews should be brought into play.*

IF YOU HAVE DONE YOUR HOMEWORK, YOU WILL HAVE A SIGNIFICANT ADVANTAGE OVER OTHERS.

Like a student graduating from college who has spent hours in placement offices preparing for his or her first serious job-hunting expedition, your Plan B has been prepared and you are ready. You have a Plan B to discuss with a superior inside of your organization or with a prospective employer outside. Study the suggestions below to learn how a Plan B can be used effectively.

| SUGGESTION 1 | **INCLUDE A SUMMARY OF YOUR PLAN B IN YOUR RESUME.** In making a job change, past history is always important. You communicate this best with a creative resume that incorporates information from your Plan B. A prospective employer may be more interested in your preparation for a new career than your previous experience or education. The best place to include your Plan B is at the very end of your resume so you can highlight what you have done to upgrade yourself recently.

---

*If you have yet to read Book II, beginning on page 77, now would be a good time to do so.

MARKETING YOUR PLAN B

SUGGESTION 2

INTRODUCE YOUR PLAN B DURING THE INTERVIEW PROCESS. Using good judgement, introduce your Plan B at the appropriate time. Explain why it was developed. Communicate how you have upgraded your skills. State how you think your Plan B prepared you to contribute more.

SUGGESTION 3

INVITE QUESTIONS ON YOUR PLAN. When a prospective employer becomes interested in your career development plan you are doing well in the interview. Rather than being asked questions that may be difficult to answer, the interviewer is asking you questions that will allow you to demonstrate you are a creative person with initiative.

SUGGESTION 4

USE THE HOME FIELD ADVANTAGE. This means that through a Plan B you may now have, (perhaps for the first time), an advantage with your present employer. Everything in your plan could help your present employer because you already know the ropes!

SUGGESTION 5

UNDERSTAND WHY YOUR PLAN B ENHANCES YOUR POTENTIAL. Anyone who completes a Plan B has demonstrated excellent potential to contribute to productivity because they have demonstrated they are pro active.

SUGGESTION 6

USE YOUR PLAN B IN A PROFESSIONAL MANNER. We earlier made the statement that when using a Plan B it is okay to play one end against the middle. In short, you can use your plan to gain the best possible position where you are now. If done openly and honestly, you can use an outside job offer as leverage to do this. Or, you can use a better ''in house'' job offer as leverage to get a better position outside. This should be done without deception so neither party will wind up with a bad taste. Although there is nothing unethical or unprofessional in keeping a Plan B undercover during the preparation period, once you use it as a vehicle to gain a better position, the veil of secrecy should be lifted and it should be used with openness and pride.

CASE #17	PLAN B SEMINARS?

Assume you are Director of Human Resources for a major firm that thus far has been able to withstand most winds of change. As a result, your employees feel rather secure and happy in their roles. Still, you are a Plan B believer. In fact, you have developed one of your own.

Known for your innovative ideas, a few days ago you started thinking about proposing to your management team the idea of having Plan B seminars. The idea appeals to you because you believe only unhappy or unproductive people would choose to leave the organization. Most would view a Plan ''B'' as a personal development program and thus make a greater contribution. The only thing that worries you is how to convince those on the team you are right.

If this were a real situation, would you take the risk? Make your decision and compare your thinking with that of the author on page 214.

IF YOU DON'T GET
STARTED ON
YOUR PLAN B
NOW (BEFORE
YOU FINISH THIS
BOOK) IT PROBABLY
WON'T HAPPEN.

PART 3

MISCONCEPTIONS ABOUT HAVING A PLAN B

MYTHS ABOUT AN ALTERNATE GROWTH PROGRAM

A PLAN B WILL DISTRACT ME FROM PLAN A: Just the opposite is likely to happen! Looking outside your present career could give it more appeal, not less. Or you might see growth opportunities you have been neglecting. In any event, one plan can help the other. Once involved, you will discover you have time and energy for both.

DOING A PLAN B IS DISCOURAGING: Many individuals think that a Plan B is distasteful. They see it as reading want ads, lining up job prospects, and doing interviews. An alternative growth program is much more than a job-hunting expedition. In fact, developing a Plan B can be exciting for four reasons: (1) You can accomplish the plan while you have the security of a regular job. (2) It is a non-stressful way to lift yourself out of a situation that is leading nowhere. (3) It provides an opportunity to take a fresh look at your future (which is probably brighter than you suspect.) (4) It can cause you to think at a higher level which, in some instances, can turn your life around.

A PLAN B IS TOO RISKY: This myth needs to be exploded quickly. Organizations recognize that employees should protect themselves from the winds of change. Upon learning that a productive employee is working on a Plan B, an enlightened manager should think: ''Perhaps we need to provide Julie with more opportunities here. If we can't, then I wish her luck elsewhere. She is entitled to her future.''

IT IS BETTER TO DO A PLAN B AS A FULL-TIME PROJECT: Some misguided individuals mistakenly believe it is better to start a growth program when they are unemployed. These people fail to recognize the security of having a Plan A (and the income that goes with it) makes it easier to design a superior plan. Outplacement counselors constantly describe the state many unemployed people fall into—a malaise that has a negative impact upon their ability to find a new position. A growth program, developed in advance, enables one to avoid this ''unemployment malaise''.

COMMON MISCONCEPTIONS

PLAN B MEANS MORE FORMAL EDUCATION: A career plan *may* require going back to school, but not always. What about those who already have the skills? Or those who want a similar job with another firm? Or those who want to improve their role through self-learning? Often a Plan B means taking advantage of Plan A learning opportunities now, so a move can be made later.

PLAN B IS FOR YOUNG AGGRESSIVE TYPES: Although a few ambitious young people may see the value of self-programming sooner, this does not mean they need it more. Just the opposite! Restructuring within a business often means the loss of upper or mid-management jobs where salaries are higher and more ''fat'' can be cut. Also, those who have been around longer may have a greater psychological need to get out of a career ''rut''. A Plan B offers the opportunity to ''break from the past'' and start over fresh.

PLAN B MEANS A GEOGRAPHICAL CHANGE: Rather than cause the uprooting of a family, a Plan B can keep you in your present home and location because of advance planning. When people lose their Plan A they often grasp at career straws that can turn their lifestyle upside down. A well-designed growth program can help a person through a major career change with a minimum of disruption. Properly perceived, a Plan B can play a major role in helping you be true to your future.

HUBIE

Hubie graduated from the business program of Ohio State University as a computer programmer. He was encouraged by his professors to join a major company as a trainee and work his way up the management ladder. After years of hard work but uneven progress, Hubie began to challenge the wisdom of his decision. Why should he confine his talents to one firm? Why should he wait to be promoted from within? Why should he hitch his future to a single corporation?

Unexpectedly, Hubie's company merged with a competitor. His job was taken by a person from the other company. Despite all of his educational preparation, productivity, and creative contributions to his company, Hubie was left out in the cold.

Why hadn't he been taught to program his own career so he could protect his future?

WHY SO MANY INDIVIDUALS NEVER DEVELOP A PLAN B

Shocking as it may seem, it is estimated that less than 3 out of every 100 workers have a well-developed alternative career plan. Reasons for this situation of "non-readiness" are many. Three of the most obvious, and understandable, are:

1. Higher education places so much emphasis on preparing students to succeed in a Plan A they neglect to point out the need for a backup program. The rationale is that you must have a successful Plan A before you are ready for a Plan B and it is not logical to do both at the same time. "Win your first career opportunity and after you have settled in, you can worry about a Plan B. First things first."

2. Many people feel there is something unethical about preparing a Plan B while on a firm's payroll. They feel it shows a lack of loyalty or honesty. On top of this some feel building a Plan B will place their Plan A in jeopardy. "If your boss discovers you are working on a alternate career possibility, she or he may take a dim view. You may have rendered yourself ineligible for promotions or fair treatment in the future. In case of a reduction, you may be the first to go." Many individuals, have yet to discover the mutual advantages of developing alternatives.

3. Perhaps the biggest reason for not developing alternative plans is that most individuals are not motivated to prepare one. It is all they can do to keep a Plan A and their home life going. They can tred water but nothing more. "Don't talk to me about something better when I am barely hanging to what I have." These individuals need to be convinced that having a Plan B will make their Plan A more comfortable while also improving their lifestyle.

WHEN IT COMES TO A PLAN A AND B, IT IS OKAY TO PLAY BOTH ENDS AGAINST THE MIDDLE*

* Providing, of course, you continue to be effective in your Plan A.

HOW WILL OTHERS REACT?

When Jessica called her sister Kim to explain how her strategy got her a higher paying, more creative position Kim replied: ''Great. When we meet next week I want to know all of the details so I can do one of my own.''

When Cody made the decision to activate his Plan B he told the whole story to his boss who replied: ''With all of the changes going on around here you did the right thing. It may come as a surprise but I am in the process of doing one of my own.''

When Dawn received a big promotion she decided to stay with her Plan A but continue to maintain her Plan B. In talking to her boss about her previously secret plan, he replied: ''I am complimented that you would discuss your plan with me and I can see now it had a lot to do with your receiving the promotion. I just hope we can continue to provide you with sufficient challenge to keep you working with us.''

SELF-TEST AHEAD

186

PRE-TEST

There are many opinions and a few misconceptions about whether a Plan B should be kept secret or communicated to co-workers or superiors. This exercise will help you make your decision. When finished, compare your answers with those below.

True   **False**

_____ _____ 1. Most people are more motivated to reach a secret goal.

_____ _____ 2. There is nothing unethical in preparing a Plan B in secret.

_____ _____ 3. Discussing a Plan B prematurely with co-workers can get it into the grapevine and be counter-productive.

_____ _____ 4. The development of a Plan B can cause one to stay with Plan A.

_____ _____ 5. This book recommends that the reader design, complete, and activate a Plan B while remaining effective with Plan A.

_____ _____ 6. Today most management people are less approving of employees with a Plan B.

_____ _____ 7. A Plan B can cause you to contribute more to an organization.

_____ _____ 8. Most people do not take it seriously when they hear someone is preparing a Plan B.

_____ _____ 9. You and you alone are responsible for your career future.

_____ _____ 10. The time will never arrive when organizations conduct Plan B seminars for their employees.

ANSWERS: 1. F (there is no evidence either way on this). **2.** T (one has the right to prepare a Plan B and it is not unethical as long as she or he remains effective with Plan A) **3.** T (one should be selective in sharing plans on the development of a Plan B). **4.** T (this is one reason why enlightened managers are often in favor of employees preparing a Plan B.) **5.** T (whether one communicates it to superiors is a personal decision). **6.** F (the "winds of change" have caused management to be more approving). **7.** T (the reason this is true will be explained later). **8.** T (this occurs because people talk about plans but few actually develop one). **9.** T (and you are free to make a change at any time). **10.** F (a few organizations conduct serious career development programs now).

THE INTRIGUE OF SECRECY

There is nothing unethical about preparing a Plan B while you continue to operate effectively in the job you were hired to perform. For several reasons, however, some individuals prefer to keep their career contingency planning undercover. They do not discuss it with co-workers or superiors. Reasons why secrecy is preferred by some individuals, include:

> "The moment I started working on a Plan B my regular job became easier and more fun. My new attitude was noticed by co-workers. A few thought I had a secret lover. Believe me I enjoyed the mystique my secrecy created."
>
> "I think one is motivated to do a better job with a Plan B when you keep your efforts secret. Knowing you are developing something which you can fall back on frees you to see things differently. You feel proud that you have the guts to do it. It is a little like being the cat that swallowed the canary."
>
> "It was nobody's fault, but when I realized I was boxed in with my Plan A, I started a Plan B. My attitude improved immediately. It was then I decided to keep it secret. I didn't want to jepordize my Plan A and was successful because I recently received a promotion."

Whether you complete your Plan B with or without communication at your Plan A work station is a personal choice. Every individual and situation is different. The approach that motivates you the most is the one recommended.

"Our plans miscarry because they have no aim. When a man does not know what harbor he is making for, no wind is the right wind."

Seneca (4 B.C.-A. D. 65)

LAUNCHING YOUR PLAN

''Man has a limited biological capacity to change. When this capacity is overwhelmed, the capacity is in future shock.''

Alvin Toffler

HAVE A PENCIL IN HAND AS YOU CONSIDER THESE SUGGESTIONS

SUGGESTION 1   First read through the MODEL on the next two pages. Although Sara Cottonwood's situation and background may not be similar to yours, you may get some ideas. You are encouraged to follow this format.

SUGGESTION 2   Start your plan now. Understand you will need to do some research later to complete it but just getting started is a big step!

SUGGESTION 3   Consult with those who constitute your support group (or others) as you proceed. View your Plan B as a major project. Six months or more may be required to complete it.

SUGGESTION 4   Be true to your self. The MODEL was designed to provide guidance in the preparation of your own special plan. Yours could be far more sophisticated and demanding.

A MODEL TO GUIDE YOU

Sara Cottonwood
Graduate Central Arkansas State University
Major: Business Administration
Special competencies: Office management and computer skills
Currently employed as Office Supervisor for Southern Supply Co., Inc.

STEP 1 COUNT DOWN

I selected Option 5 because my close friend and co-worker Margaret and I will work together. We plan to have dinner together every Tuesday after work and share the progress we are making.

STEP 2 HEDGE YOUR BET

I checked 8 of the streamlining suggestions and will follow through on them in the next few weeks. In addition, I intend to do the following.

    Delegate more to others in my office.
    Make a list of daily priorities so that
        I have a minimum of 30 minutes each
        noon hour to work on my Plan B.
    Ask my superior to assign my credit union
        responsibilities to another manager.
    Demonstrate more leadership so others will
        not flood me with work they should be
        doing themselves.

STEP 3 YOU'VE GOT TO BE KIDDING!

I have isolated the following learning opportunities where I work and pursue them when time permits and the situation is right.

Negotiation Strategies Workshop March 6th & 7th
Leadership Seminar April 16th
Word Processing Software, Learn via company tutorial

SARA COTTONWOOD'S PLAN B

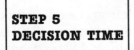

**STEP 4
QUALIFY FIRST!**

Here are the competency standards that I intend to reach during the next six months.

Upgrade computer application skills in the area of word processing and data base management

Improve my communication and counseling skills

**STEP 5
DECISION TIME**

Each semester until my Plan B is complete I will enroll at the university for courses in database management. Successful completion of these courses will make me proficient in the latest generation of relational databases.

I recognize that I need to improve my management skills so I will do this both by attending company seminars and at night on a self-paced basis. I will subscribe to: OFFICE MANAGEMENT

**STEP 6
CREATIVE
NETWORKING**

I plan to build my network on an ongoing basis. I intend to add one person per week to a list composed of key individuals. Each will be in a position to give me both guidance and contacts. I anticipate at least 50% of these key people will come from my trade group (NOMA). To improve my accessibility to such people I intend to become an officer in that association. I now have three people on my list. I hope to wind up with 15.

**STEP 7
HAVE PLAN—
WILL TRAVEL**

Although I may change my mind when the time arrives, I plan to activate my Plan B when it is finished. I like the challenge of doing this while I continue to make progress with my present firm. My goal is to increase my annual income by $10,000.00 or more (with comparable benefits). When the time is right I will speed up my networking and use my Plan B for both information and actual job interviews. Frankly, I am more excited about the future than at any time since I graduated from college seven years ago. Margaret feels the same way.

Wish me luck!

PLAN B WORKSHEETS

START NOW AND FINISH LATER

Your name: _____

Anticipated date of completion: _____

| **STEP 1 COUNT DOWN** | I am going with Option #_____. My reasons are: _____ |

_____

| **STEP 2 HEDGE YOUR BET** | To free myself to develop my Plan B I intend to streamline my present job in the following ways: |

_____

_____

_____

_____

| **STEP 3 YOU'VE GOT TO BE KIDDING!** | I have isolated the following learning opportunities where I work. |

_____

_____

_____

_____

WORKSHEETS (Continued)

| STEP 4 QUALIFY FIRST! | Here are the competency standards that I intend to reach. |

_____

_____

_____

| STEP 5 DECISION TIME | I will enroll in and complete the following courses: |

_____

_____

_____

My self-help learning program at home will include:

_____

_____

_____

| STEP 6 CREATIVE NETWORKING | My networking strategy will be. I will or will not use the endless chain networking system. |

_____

_____

_____

| STEP 7 HAVE PLAN— WILL TRAVEL | Whether or not I activate my Plan B when completed will depend upon: |

_____

_____

_____

WHEN DOUBTS REMAIN

It is natural for some readers to remain skeptical about the Plan B concept. Is it really worth all of the time and effort? Would there really be a substantial payoff for me?

Obviously, you must find agreement within yourself on the value of a Plan B. To help you do this, three hypothetical cases are presented. Please read, react, and then compare your views with those of the author.

CASE #18	JEREMY & PAUL

Jeremy and Paul's relationship was work oriented. They have been in the same department, doing the same basic work for four years. Although both are the same age, have similar backgrounds, and are married with children, they did not see each other socially.

Last year rumors persisted that their firm would go through a major restructuring and some departments would be eliminated. Jeremy took the rumors seriously and encouraged Paul to do the same. In fact, he suggested they help each other develop a Plan B. Paul showed no interest, so Jeremy independently started work on one. Among other things, it included going back to school to upgrade his skills and the beginnings of a job search.

When the announcement was made that their department had been eliminated, Paul was in a state of shock. He asked Jeremy to have a beer with him that afternoon. "Jer", said Paul, "I'm really scared about the future. In addition to our mortgage, we owe on our cars and have other bills. I guess we should have taken those rumors seriously." Jeremy replied: "I did, Paul but you will recall you were not interested at the time. Let me tell you what I have been doing and perhaps it may help you get started."

Is it too late for Paul to do a Plan B? Please write out your answer in the spaces provided and turn to page 214 to compare your views.

_____

_____

_____

_____

_____

CASE #19

GERALDINE

Gerry, newly employed by Trac Corporation, was discouraged by the complacency of her more experienced co-workers. Sensing that her future was limited at Trac, she started work on a Plan B. A major part of her strategy was to take advantage of her present job by learning more. She asked to learn how to operate the latest equipment. She asked for more responsibility when new programs were introduced. This helped provide more knowledge and contributed to her positive attitude. Gerry kept her personal productivity high, not to impress her superiors, but to prepare herself for another career opportunity.

One morning, to her surprise, Geraldine was invited into the division manager's office and offered the position of department manager. The new position would give her a 20% increase in salary and new opportunities to learn.

Is this case realistic? Is it possible that in preparing for a better job elsewhere an employee can receive an unusual opportunity at home? Please express your views and compare with those of the author on page 214

_____

_____

_____

_____

_____

CASE #20	LARRY

Almost everyone around the plant knew about the conflict between Larry and his boss. Unfortunately, it was so hard on Larry that he required professional help. Things started to get better only after the counselor suggested that Larry start making plans to free himself from a situation that was untenable for both he and his family.

It came as no surprise when Larry resigned. What did surprise everyone was hearing that Larry had developed a Plan B and had an offer to join a competitive organization with a superior position. In discussing the situation later with a former colleague, Larry said: "It was obvious months ago that I could not build a good relationship so I took the only door open to me. I kept learning and protecting myself while I did some upgrading and serious networking. Do I have hard feelings? Just the opposite. Without the problem I would not have been motivated to do a Plan B in the first place."

What was the real advantage of a Plan B to Larry? Please write out your answer and compare with that found on page 214.

_____

_____

_____

_____

_____

MAINTENANCE IDEAS!

We earlier compared a Plan B to an insurance policy or having money wisely invested. When it comes to maintaining a completed Plan B it might be best to compare it to a fine automobile. Just like any mechanical device, a plan can deteriorate and become inoperative if not used properly or neglected.

To maintain an automobile you must put in gas and oil, get an occasional lube job and keep the engine tuned. Now and then some repairs will be necessary. To maintain a Plan B you must keep your skills at high standards, continue your networking efforts, schedule information interviews on a regular basis, and review and revise your Plan B as required. Your Plan B shouldn't gather cobwebs.

Listed below are some Plan B maintenance tips. Please place a ☑ opposite those you intend to honor.

☐ Keep your plan and this book in a prominent place as a reminder that you have the equivalent of a career insurance policy providing you keep your Plan B up to date.

☐ Thumb through your plan every three months to see if deletions or additions need to be made.

☐ Remind yourself that your plan is, in effect, your mental health protection plan. It provides you with both freedom and security.

☐ Your plan should pay your interest. That is, it should provide you with psychological dividends like increased motivation, confidence, and a greater willingness to take risks.

☐ One of the best ways to maintain a Plan B is to help someone else do one. In doing this, you may discover a weakness in your own.

☐ An ideal time to do a "maintenance check" is when you return from a professional meeting or trade conference. New trends, compentency standards, and additions to your network should be added.

COMMON MISTAKES

Four common mistakes are listed below. Now that you have almost finished this book, which one are you most apt to make? Place a ☑ in the appropriate box.

☐ **UNDERESTIMATING THE EXCITEMENT AND INTRIGUE INVOLVED.** Many people consider developing and maintaining a Plan B as work. They are wrong. Like taking a first trip in a balloon, a well developed plan can provide a new perspective on your career and future. This happens because you free yourself from organizational dependency. It's a greet feeling!

☐ **FIGURING YOU HAVE A PLAN WHEN YOU DON'T.** Now that you know what is involved (seven steps) you may not make this mistake. Still, you may be tempted to take too many shortcuts. You do not want to pay premiums on an insurance policy that you can't collect on when the chips are down.

☐ **WAITING TOO LONG TO GET STARTED.** If you were to receive notice today that your job will be eliminated in 30 days you waited too long. Few good plans can be prepared and completed in less than three months.

☐ **REFUSING TO SEE THE FULL VALUE.** Some people persist in thinking that a Plan B does little more than win you a promotion or another job. In addition, a true plan can enhance your Plan A, contribute to fulfilling your life goals, and provide you with a new, exciting philosophy of work.

SELF-QUIZ

Please answer the following true-false questions.

TRUE	FALSE

_____   _____   1. You can't have a Plan B without a Plan A.

_____   _____   2. The value of a Plan B does not depend upon whether or not it is exercised.

_____   _____   3. Having a secret Plan B is unethical.

_____   _____   4. A Plan B will provide you with the career you should have chosen years ago.

_____   _____   5. The farther you fall behind in job skills of your specialty the longer it will take you to complete a Plan B.

_____   _____   6. Networking is building strong mutually rewarding relationships with people who are in a position to help you activate your Plan B when it is ready.

_____   _____   7. An information interview is designed to keep you in touch with the job market and those competencies required.

_____   _____   8. Networking and information interviews are a minor part of developing a Plan B.

_____   _____   9. A Plan B frequently sends the preparer back to college.

_____   _____   10. Some individuals improve their skills through assuming more responsibility in their current job.

SELF-QUIZ (Continued)

TRUE	FALSE	
_____	_____	11. Self-learning at home can sometimes contribute as much to a successful Plan B as formal learning on campus.
_____	_____	12. A good time to construct a Plan B is while you are drawing unemployment insurance.
_____	_____	13. The moment your Plan B is operational it becomes your Plan A and you need another Plan B.
_____	_____	14. The best way to make yourself more ''marketable'' is to improve your job skills.
_____	_____	15. The three best ways to improve your special competencies are to: (1) learn more at your present job (2) take college courses (3) engage in self-learning at home.
_____	_____	16. Once a Plan B is complete it does not require maintenance for at least a year.
_____	_____	17. A Plan B is essentially a philosophy toward work.
_____	_____	18. Many colleges now offer seminars on the significance of having a Plan B and how to develop one.
_____	_____	19. Lack of motivation is the number one reason most people do not have a Plan B.
_____	_____	20. Restructuring, mergers, and relocations are a passing fad and will slow down in the future.

SELF-QUIZ (Continued)

TRUE	FALSE	
_____	_____	21. It is estimated that less than 3% of those employed full-time have a workable Plan B.
_____	_____	22. The program presented in this book contains a seven-step process that can be completed in a few weeks.
_____	_____	23. Doing a Plan B is all work and no play.
_____	_____	24. The endless chain system is an interviewing technique.
_____	_____	25. A Plan B is designed to improve your Plan A while it prepares you to lose it.

EACH CORRECT ANSWER IS WORTH FOUR POINTS.

TOTAL SCORE ☐

(Correct answers on the following page.)

ANSWERS TO SELF-QUIZ

COMPARE YOUR ANSWERS WITH THOSE OF THE AUTHOR:

1. TRUE — A plan A is your present career role, a Plan B is an alternative yet to be exercised.
2. TRUE — Sometimes developing a Plan B motivates one to do a better job with Plan A and a promotion makes it undesirable to move.
3. FALSE — There is nothing unethical about protecting your future from the modern winds of change.
4. FALSE — Finding the right career is a separate matter. A Plan B, however, can lead you in the right direction.
5. TRUE — When you fall too far behind going back to college may be necessary and this takes time.
6. TRUE — Advance networking is a critical part of any Plan B.
7. TRUE — This is necessary so you will know when your Plan B is complete and operational.
8. FALSE — A major part!
9. TRUE — Taking a college course (or earning a degree) is often the only way to reach one's Plan B goals.
10. TRUE — These are very perceptive and smart individuals.
11. TRUE — Self-learning at home is on the increase. More publications are available.
12. FALSE — You can't do a Plan B without a Plan A.
13. TRUE — This means you may develop more than one Plan B.
14. TRUE — In most fields, skill improvement (retraining) is increasingly necessary.
15. TRUE — Steps 5, 6, & 7 in the Plan B process.
16. FALSE — Like maintaining an automobile, frequent repairs and tuning are required.
17. TRUE — A Plan B has both a pragmatic and philosophical side.
18. FALSE — Hopefully they may do so in the future.
19. TRUE — Most people talk Plan B but actually do little in constructing one.
20. FALSE — Most experts believe the trend will continue for at least ten years—perhaps to the next century.
21. TRUE — The author believes this low percentage figure will increase substantially in the next few years.
22. FALSE — Seven steps, yes; but there is too much involved to complete a good plan in a few weeks.
23. FALSE — Doing a plan can and should also be fun.
24. FALSE — The ''endless chain'' system is a networking technique.
25. TRUE — This is a paradox some find difficult to accept.

APPENDIX I

USING THE PLAN B APPROACH TO WIN THE RIGHT PART-TIME RETIREMENT JOB.

A growing number of individuals over 50 have lost jobs due to the winds of change. Others are unhappy because of human conflicts and/or the downgrading of their responsibilities. Still others realize they need job involvement after retirement for either financial or psychological reasons. The result of all this is that many employees within distance of retirement need a special kind of Plan B.

Although highly qualified in the field of printing and graphics Lee, at 53, is finding it difficult to locate a challenging replacement. His previous position was eliminated. Result? He is developing a Plan B that will move him into retirement sooner than he and his wife had anticipated.

Ruth, a widow of 60, needs to supplement her retirement income. Result? She is learning new skills and upgrading old ones to find a part-time job that will take her to 65 and Medicare coverage.

Ken is 55 and under great pressure from a superior who would like nothing better than to see him retire. Result? Tired of waiting for a ''golden handshake'', Ken is busy working on a Plan B that will provide additional retirement income through a part-time job.

Notice that neither Lee, Ruth, or Ken *desire* a full time job after retirement. All have a financial package sufficient to make do providing they can create a supplemental income that falls within their comfort zones. For many people, this is a most difficult challenge. They want to work, but not full time. They want a job, but one with less pressure. They want a position with some dignity and which will provide enough income or creative involvement to make it worthwhile. Research shows that many financially secure retirees still need some form of work to keep them challenged.

LAST CHANCE TO BE TRUE TO YOUR FUTURE

Retirement is the last chance an individual has to be true to his or her future. Finding the *right* part-time position is critical. In some cases this may mean doing a late-in-life career search to find a fresh, creative career. For example, many retirees go into business for themselves. Those who elect to work for others need all the job-finding skills of a recent college graduate. Perhaps more.

NOTHING MAKES MORE SENSE THAN USING THE SEVEN STEP PLAN B PROCESS. For example, assume you would like to retire next year from your current job (Plan A) but will need a challenging part-time job (for either money or psychological reasons). If you return to page xx and go through the seven steps a second time, you will see (with some variations) just how applicable the process can be to your special situation. To assist you in doing this, the seven steps are adjusted and augmented below. It is suggested you read the step in the body of the text first and then read the suggestions below.

STEP 1: COUNT DOWN. Face it, you need as much support in preparing a retirement program as you do for a Plan B. Maybe more! Your best approach would be to sign up for a pre-retirement seminar (if your company does not offer one you might enroll in one at a local college). This could become a support group for you. Your Plan B effort would give your comprehensive retirement plan special help in an area where it is most needed. If married, it is strongly recommended that you work as a team with your spouse. Other support people may also be needed.

EACH STEP WORKS!

STEP 2: HEDGE YOUR BET. There are two reasons why, as a possible retiree you should consider streamlining your job. First, simplify things at work to get rid of some pressure. This is traditional and often expected by employers. Second, you need extra time (both on the job and at home) to do retirement planning. The more efficient you become at work, the more excited you will be about retirement! Go to it!

STEP 3: YOU'VE GOT TO BE KIDDING. Just because you are thinking about retirement is not a signal for you to stop learning. Just the opposite! Now is the time to learn skills from your present job that will help you qualify for a post-retirement job. Can you transfer present skills or do you need to learn new ones? What can you learn now that will help you later? It is natural for people about to retire to stop learning. This is never wise. Give this step some thought!

STEP 4: QUALIFY FIRST. Many people who retire are forced to take part-time jobs beneath their capabilities. This, of course, is free choice (some like getting away from the pressures). Most retirees however want a mental challenge and the financial rewards that go along with accomplishments. If this sounds like you, then the time to qualify for a new career or position is while you are still on a payroll. The way to do this, of course, is to find the job you really want ahead of time. Then start the qualification process. This is especially true if you intend to start your own business.

IT'S NEVER TOO LATE!

STEP 5: DECISION TIME. More and more individuals approaching retirement are returning to college to learn new skills or bring old ones up to date. Some plan to turn hobbies into part-time endeavors. Others will learn skills so they can build boats, homes, or do repair work at their own pace. Still others will develop office skills so they can find part-time jobs near their homes. If a local university or community college does not offer what is needed, self-instruction is often the answer. Some will do limited moonlighting, (like working as a small appliance repair person two or three nights per week).

STEP 6: CREATIVE NETWORKING. Everything in this step applies to a potential retiree! Although an employment agency might come up with the kind of part-time job you seek, it is unlikely because most agencies work primarily with those seeking full-time jobs. Thus it is more important for you to take the initiative. Through networking and information interviews you need to determine the job situation you desire. This means maintaining your confidence and not selling yourself short because of age. Also, do not permit prospective employers to take advantage of you with lower wages than deserved or expectation of more work than is reasonable. Networking is the answer and the sooner you start the better!

STEP 7: HAVE PLAN-WILL TRAVEL. As a soon to be retiree, you may not want to travel (where you decide to retire is usually more important than any part-time job). Your Plan B will be the key. In keeping an information or employment interview, simply tell your contact what you plan to do. Ask if anything fits both your needs and theirs.

Of course, ''The Proof Is In The Pudding.'' The seven steps provide strategy, but only you can develop a written plan and implement it.

As you do this, you may wish to use the best selling book COMFORT ZONES; A PRACTICAL GUIDE TO RETIREMENT PLANNING as a resource to your retirement planning. COMFORT ZONES is a complete guide to retirement (it covers both financial and emotional aspects) and can be ordered from CRISP PUBLICATIONS, 95 First Street, Los Altos, California 94022 for just $15.00 which includes postage.

AUTHOR'S SUGGESTED ANSWERS TO CASES

CASE 1: A PROBLEM FOR JOYCE

Joyce has a classic career-lifestyle conflict. If she pursues her career as an executive, it will be difficult to enjoy the lifestyle she seems to want. On the other hand, she may have to accept a career that is not her first choice to live in the environment she prefers. Countless people face this same problem every day. The author believes Joyce can reach her goal as an executive and still pretty much lead the lifestyle she wishes. It will probably not happen in the beginning; but once Joyce has enjoyed some success, she can live in a rural-life setting and commute.

CASE 2: JAKE'S DILEMMA

Even with Jake's determination and a strong tutor, it is doubtful whether or not he would earn an engineering degree. Jake must understand the difference between theoretical engineers and practical engineers. Jake falls in the latter classification. Here, he could be successful and probably would be happier. It would probably be better for Jake to take a demanding two-year technical program, than place himself under the pressure required in going after an engineering degree. There is a danger that Jake may become so discouraged he will throw in the educational towel and injure his future.

CASE 3: WILL JOE FIND THE RIGHT CAREER?

If Joe sticks with his plan, he probably will do fine.

It would be best, however, if Joe invested time in a "Career Search" class (with or without credit) so his search process would be more structured. Also, he would gain appropriate reinforcement from his teacher and fellow students. Most people who initiate a career-finding program never fully complete it. Joe is to be congratulated for trying to select a career on his own. It is estimated that only a small percentage of those in college make any serious attempt to systematically select a career.

CASE 4: MID-LIFE CAREER CHANGE

Once Richard leaves his current job, a good way to select which entrepreneurial path to follow is to continue living where they are and find a way to work part-time in each of the prospective work environments. Whenever it is possible to test out a career environment by becoming a part of it, a better decision can usually be made.

CASE 5: SECOND THOUGHTS

When it comes to a career choice, second thoughts are natural and should be expected. If Mrs. Henderson did a conscientious job, her misgivings may not be justified; and she should have confidence in CAREER DISCOVERY as well as in her own decision-making ability.

Mrs. Henderson should be encouraged to do a more in-depth search if she has the time. Such a search may eliminate some of her misgivings. It is possible she could come up with a choice different from that of Psychiatric Nurse.

AUTHOR'S SUGGESTED ANSWERS TO CASES
(Continued)

Mrs. Henderson should, also, be encouraged to complete CAREER DISCOVERY a second time. It is vital she be totally committed to her choice before she begins the difficult educational workload necessary to reach her goal.

CASE 6: WHO HAS THE ADVANTAGE?

The author feels the advantage between Janet and Christy is almost equal. Those with jobs can usually maintain a more positive attitude during the search period. Also, some firms prefer hiring individuals currently employed. Christy has the advantage however of being able to put her full efforts into a search. She can get closer to the available opportunities, and complete more interviews. The longer Christy is unemployed, however, the greater Janet's advantage. It is often a good idea to take an interim job while continuing the search for the best opportunity.

CASE 7: WHO WILL GET THE BEST JOB?

Although Frank could luck out and find an excellent job, Wayne's approach makes more sense. Many job applicants who attempt to find a job too quickly wind up dissatisfied. This is especially true of new graduates who are so anxious to find something they succumb to their own pressures and make a premature choice. Although Frank might be able to pull off some excellent interviews (he seems to have a popular personality and lots of confidence), Wayne, over a three-month period, should have a better opportunity to perfect his techniques.

CASE 8: WHICH PROSPECTING SYSTEM IS BEST?

Although there may be exceptions, Mary's weekly plan contains more logic than Jessie's, and would be easier to put into practice. It is true that flexibility has advantages, but too little structure often results in taking the easy way out and doing nothing. Setting up interviews—and winning the best job—is hard work. If Mary sticks with her plan she will, eventually, enjoy success. Most potential employers are pleased to schedule interviews a few days in advance.

CASE 9: WHICH RESUME STRATEGY IS SUPERIOR?

Rose has a more balanced marketing plan. Jake is putting too much faith in a single mailing. In most situations, it takes the right combination of personal effort plus a selective use of resumes to win interviews with the right organizations.

CASE 10: WHO WILL REMAIN POSITIVE LONGEST?

The author likes Sam's plan best for two reasons. First, he plans to stay busier by working four days a week. Experience shows that too little activity can cause "down periods." Second, he recognizes he needs a human support system during the period. If Grace would spend more time on her search and develop a better human support system, her plan would also be an excellent one.

CASE 11: RICHARD

If both Richard and his wife Marie are giving consideration to the Uncle George possibility, it seems that Marie questions her ability to provide enough motivation. If Uncle George is the best "model" Richard has available, and if Uncle George is willing to go with an informal contract, the author feels this might be the best motivator. This arrangement would be less complex to start with and easier for Richard to maintain. Although Richard can communicate his plan to the other people (and they can be of help along the way) his commitment to Uncle George could provide 90% of the motivation required.

CASE 12: CONFLICT

James does not see the long-range, true value of a Plan B. He refuses to see that he can make changes now that will help him no matter what happens in the future. James subscribes to the old-fashioned theory that the only way to get a better job is to dump your present one first. Gregg believes you can use a present job, no matter how unpleasant it may be, to gain a better one.

CASE 13: ATTITUDE REVERSAL

It is doubtful that Tanya will be able to turn things around in her present job. Because of this, it might be best for her not to expect so much from herself but rather do other things to prepare a Plan B. Although it is best to make all possible improvements with Plan A while working on Plan B, all of the major behavioral reverses she must make are not realistic.

CASE 14: JACK'S PROBLEM

It depends just how much improvement Jack must make to bring his skills up to standard. If the gap is extremely wide, it might be best for him to return to campus full time. Once caught up, Jack can try for a fresh start. If, however, the gap is modest, Jack's three step approach can work and will produce less strain on himself.

AUTHOR'S SUGGESTED ANSWERS TO CASES
(Continued)

CASE 15: CHALLENGE FOR MARY

Mary is lucky that she has such a good opportunity to carve out a practical career for herself. She should find out, however how long it would be before she could be transferred into the marketing department. The combination of college work, self-study, and on-the-job learning is ideal. With Mary's background, progress should be speedy.

CASE 16: THE CONTACT THAT PAID OFF

Hazel is expressing sour grapes because she has never given networking a chance. True, networking can lead one up blind alleys, but it only takes one right contact to wind up a winner. Donna is to be congratulated for being so persistant.

CASE 17: PLAN B SEMINARS

The author is of the opinion that any large organization, especially one that is downsizing, would benefit from offering employees such a seminar. There would be some exceptions, but generally speaking helping people develop a Plan B would increase productivity and encourage them to remain rather than leave.

CASE 18: JEREMY & PAUL

It is not too late for Paul to get started on finding a new job but it is too late for him to prepare a Plan B. The reader is reminded that a Plan B is developed ahead of time while the individual still has a Plan A. Jeremy stands a chance of finding a better job. Paul may have to initially settle for something beneath his previous responsibilities.

CASE 19: GERALDINE

The author contends that this case is highly realistic because Geraldine's Plan B caused her to live up to her potential while the other employees drifted along. Thus Geraldine's performance stood out. It was not important for management to know Geraldine has a Plan B.

CASE 20: LARRY

When Larry started to develop a departure plan he kept himself from being victimized. Without a plan, Larry could have become so bitter and frustrated that he would have been damaged. A Plan B can help one do a better job of surviving until a new opportunity opens up. Sometimes a Plan B is the only way to turn a bad situation into an excellent one.

NOTES

NOTES

NOTES

NOTES

NOTES

NOTES

ABOUT BE TRUE TO YOUR FUTURE

The author of this book has written three individual companion volumes titled
CAREER DISCOVERY, I GOT THE JOB! and PLAN B: PROTECTING YOUR CAREER FROM THE WINDS OF CHANGE. These titles are in the ''Fifty-Minute'' format and may be ordered using the form on page 223.

These three books represent a continuum that allows a reader to establish a life goal and select a career based on it (CAREER DISCOVERY), find the best available job within that career (I GOT THE JOB!) and stay competitive in that job (PLAN B: PROTECTING YOUR CAREER FROM THE WINDS OF CHANGE).

Learn for yourself why this series can help you develop better life planning skills.

ABOUT THE FIFTY-MINUTE SERIES

''Fifty-Minute books are the best new publishing idea in years. They are clear, practical, concise and affordable — perfect for today's world.''

Leo Hauser
(Past President, ASTD)

What Is A Fifty-Minute Book?

—Fifty-Minute books are brief, soft-cover, ''self-study'' modules which cover a single concept. They are reasonably priced, and ideal for formal training programs, excellent for self-study and perfect for remote location training.

Why Are Fifty-Minute Books Unique?

—Because of their format and level. Designed to be ''read with a pencil,'' the basics of a subject can be quickly grasped and applied through a series of hands-on activities, exercises and cases.

How Many Fifty-Minute Books Are There?

—Those listed on page 223 at this time, however, additional titles are in development. For more information write to **Crisp Publications, Inc., 95 First Street, Los Altos, CA 94022.**

THE FIFTY-MINUTE SERIES

Quantity	Title	Code #	Price	Amount
	The Fifty-Minute Supervisor—*2nd Edition*	58-0	$6.95	
	Effective Performance Appraisals—*Revised*	11-4	$6.95	
	Successful Negotiation—*Revised*	09-2	$6.95	
	Quality Interviewing—*Revised*	13-0	$6.95	
	Team Building: An Exercise in Leadership—*Revised*	16-5	$7.95	
	Performance Contracts: The Key To Job Success—*Revised*	12-2	$6.95	
	Personal Time Management	22-X	$6.95	
	Effective Presentation Skills	24-6	$6.95	
	Better Business Writing	25-4	$6.95	
	Quality Customer Service	17-3	$6.95	
	Telephone Courtesy & Customer Service	18-1	$6.95	
	Restaurant Server's Guide To Quality Service—*Revised*	08-4	$6.95	
	Sales Training Basics—*Revised*	02-5	$6.95	
	Personal Counseling—*Revised*	14-9	$6.95	
	Balancing Home & Career	10-6	$6.95	
	Mental Fitness: A Guide To Emotional Health	15-7	$6.95	
	Attitude: Your Most Priceless Possession	21-1	$6.95	
	Preventing Job Burnout	23-8	$6.95	
	Successful Self-Management	26-2	$6.95	
	Personal Financial Fitness	20-3	$7.95	
	Job Performance and Chemical Dependency	27-0	$7.95	
	Career Discovery—*Revised*	07-6	$6.95	
	Study Skills Strategies—*Revised*	05-X	$6.95	
	I Got The Job!—*Revised*	59-9	$6.95	
	Effective Meetings Skills	33-5	$7.95	
	The Business of Listening	34-3	$6.95	
	Professional Sales Training	42-4	$7.95	
	Customer Satisfaction: The Other Half of Your Job	57-2	$7.95	
	Managing Disagreement Constructively	41-6	$7.95	
	Professional Excellence for Secretaries	52-1	$6.95	
	Starting A Small Business: A Resource Guide	44-0	$7.95	
	Developing Positive Assertiveness	38-6	$6.95	
	Writing Fitness-Practical Exercises for Better Business Writing	35-1	$7.95	
	An Honest Day's Work: Motivating Employees to Give Their Best	39-4	$6.95	
	Marketing Your Consulting & Professional Services	40-8	$7.95	
	Time Management On The Telephone	53-X	$6.95	
	Training Managers to Train	43-2	$7.95	
	New Employee Orientation	46-7	$6.95	
	The Art of Communicating: Achieving Impact in Business	45-9	$7.95	
	Technical Presentation Skills	55-6	$7.95	
	Plan B: Protecting Your Career from the Winds of Change	48-3	$7.95	
	A Guide To Affirmative Action	54-8	$7.95	
	Memory Skills in Business	56-4	$6.95	

(Continued on next page)

THE FIFTY-MINUTE SERIES
(Continued)

☐ Send volume discount information.

☐ Add my name to CPI's mailing list.

	Amount
Total (from other side)	
Shipping ($1.50 first book, $.50 per title thereafter)	
California Residents add 7% tax	
Total	

Ship to: _____

_____

_____

_____

Phone number: _____

Bill to: _____

_____

_____

_____

P.O. # _____

**All orders except those with a P.O.# must be prepaid.
Call (415) 949-4888 for more information.**

‖‖‖

C   27